CW00410997

2004

GEMINI
2004

GEMINI
2004

Jane Struthers

p

This is a Parragon Book
First published in 2003

Parragon
Queen Street House
4 Queen Street
Bath BA1 1HE
UK

Produced by Magpie Books, an imprint of
Constable & Robinson Ltd, London

© Jane Struthers 2003

Illustrations courtesy of Slatter-Anderson, London
Cover courtesy of Simon Levy

All rights reserved. This book is sold subject to the condition
that it shall not, by way of trade or otherwise, be lent, re-sold,
hired out or otherwise circulated in any form of binding or
cover other than that in which it is published and without a
similar condition including this condition being imposed on
the subsequent purchaser.

ISBN 1-40541-564-9

A copy of the British Library Cataloguing-in-Publication Data
is available from the British Library

Printed and bound in the EU

CONTENTS

Dates for 2004

Gemini 22 May – 21 June

Cancer 22 June – 22 July

Leo 23 July – 23 August

Virgo 24 August – 23 September

Libra 24 September – 23 October

Scorpio 24 October – 22 November

Sagittarius 23 November – 21 December

Capricorn 22 December – 20 January

Aquarius 21 January – 18 February

Pisces 19 February – 20 March

Aries 21 March – 20 April

Taurus 21 April – 21 May

INTRODUCTION

Dear Gemini

Happy New Year! I hope that 2004 is everything you want it to be, and more. If you're a clever Gemini you'll want to make the very best of the opportunities coming your way in the year ahead, which is why this book is so useful. It will help you to maximize your many chances and show you how to deal with any problem areas that you encounter.

My summary of 2004 in **The Year 2004** tells you exactly what you can expect in your relationships, health, money and career this year, and how to make the most of them. This is followed by my day-by-day forecasts for 2004, complete with at-a-glance charts that show you the general trend for each month.

Being born under the sign of Gemini gives you a special set of characteristics, and you can read all about them in **Your Gemini Sun Sign**. It's divided into four sections describing your relationships, health, money and career, so you can get a thorough insight into your personality. If some of your relationships have been puzzling you recently, you need to read **Love and the Stars** to discover what's going on. It describes your compatibility with each of the twelve signs, and is followed by two charts that show how you get on with the other signs in love and sex, and also as friends.

Everyone needs to get away from it all every now and then, and holidays can be good for our health. If you've ever wondered which is the ideal holiday for your Gemini Sun sign, turn to **Your Astrological Holiday Guide** to discover which destinations and activities will suit you best.

If you were born at the beginning or end of Gemini you may have always wondered if you're really a Gemini or whether you're a Taurean or Cancerian instead. Well, you can finally solve the mystery by turning to **Born on the Cusp?** and discovering which is your true Sun sign.

This book is all you need to get the very best out of 2004, so have fun and make it a great year!

Jane Struthers

THE YEAR 2004

 Friends and Lovers

You're going to have a bumper year, and there will be plenty of enjoyment with both your family and your friends. Your family life will occupy a lot of your time between January and late September, and it's a great opportunity to bask in the company of your nearest and dearest. If some of your relatives live a long way away, you might even be inspired to organize a reunion for them all, in which case you'll enjoy taking care of even the smallest details. There could also be an addition to the family in 2004, whether it's the arrival of a new baby or someone who marries into the clan.

From the end of September onwards, you'll get even more happiness than usual from being with some of your favourite people. You'll also be very popular so might find it hard to fit in as many social engagements as you'd like because there simply aren't enough hours in the day. Don't underestimate the personal magnetism you'll be exuding, especially if you're currently a solo Gemini who's looking for a kindred spirit. You might be swept off your feet by Mr or Ms Right towards the end of the year.

Unfortunately, not every relationship has brought you un-alloyed joy in recent years and you've had some difficult encounters with certain people. Sadly, that trend continues in 2004 but it will teach you a great deal about yourself in the process, especially if you're able to consider why you're having such spectacular personality clashes at the moment. Maybe the people you're falling out with are quite similar to you in some ways, although you don't want to believe it. Recognizing some of the more difficult aspects of your own character will help you to be more accepting of other people, which can only lead to improvements in all your relationships.

Health

Throughout the year it's important for you to find ways to relax. Unwinding is often difficult for Geminis at the best of times, and this is a year in which you'll find that you're coiled up like a spring every now and then. Activities with a spiritual or mystical slant, such as meditation, will help you to calm down, and will also give added meaning to your life.

If something is worrying you, it's important that you talk about it to someone or find other ways to get your problems into perspective. Devote plenty of time to your priorities in life, especially if they have nothing to do with your job or your responsibilities. Paying attention to your values, and giving them the respect you think they're due, will make you feel good and help you through any difficult patches you encounter.

From late September onwards, life will offer you many enjoyments and you'll feel much more light-hearted. There could be a lot of partying going on, if you're lucky, but although this will be fun it may not do your waistline much good. So try not to eat and drink as though it's going out of style, or you could find that there's more of you at the end of the year than there was at the beginning!

Money

Want to make your money work for you in 2004? Then invest it in domestic items or bricks and mortar. For instance, if you're fed up with your current kitchen you might decide to revamp it or even rip it out and start again. Moving house might be on the cards, too, in which case it will be a canny thing to do and you'll end up with a terrific investment. If you're in the happy position of having money to spare, you might consider buying some antiques.

However, it's very important that you don't fritter away your cash in 2004, even if you think you'll have an endless supply of the stuff. Ideally, you should stash away some of it for a rainy day, just in case you need it. There is a chance of delays or hassles if you're waiting to receive some money, in which case it will be good to know you can draw on your savings if needs be. If you do encounter some financially lean patches in 2004 it will be easy to fret about them but try to keep your worries in proportion because chewing your fingernails down to the quick won't actually achieve anything and might even distract you from taking constructive action.

All in all, this is an excellent year for developing some good financial habits, such as being very responsible when handling your money or saving regular amounts of cash each month.

Career

It's going to be quite a year! In fact, you might look back on this as a turning point in your life, in which you develop more of your many talents, branch out in new directions and show how innovative you can be in the right circumstances.

If you're bored with your current job or career, what's to stop you changing it? Don't assume that you're stuck with it for life because you could be in for a big surprise, with major changes on the horizon in 2004. This is especially likely if you were born between 21 and 28 May. You might find that you're being steered into uncharted waters, which will turn out to be really exciting.

This is a year for trusting in your plans for the future, particularly in the second half of April when it's a very auspicious period for turning dreams into reality. Don't dismiss some of your ideas as being too far-fetched because you won't know what you're capable of achieving until you give it a try. The second half of October is another very providential phase for you, with plenty of opportunities to shine. Good luck, Gemini!

Your Day by Day Guide

JANUARY AT A GLANCE

Love	♥ ♥
Money	£ $ £ $ £
Career	💻 💻 💻
Health	☼ ☼

• *Thursday 1 January* •

Happy New Year! If you were up half the night celebrating you're probably telling yourself that today's rather lacklustre mood is all because you didn't get enough sleep. Yet it may be more than that, such as a lurking doubt about the validity of some of your plans and the support you can expect from certain people. Right now you have a tendency to look on the gloomy side when things don't go the way you want, but do what you can to remain positive. There's so much for you to look forward to, Gemini!

• *Friday 2 January* •

You're in a much better mood today, thank goodness. You'll appreciate having some privacy, especially if you want to reflect on everything that 2003 brought you and look ahead to 2004. An in-depth discussion with someone you trust and love will help you to marshal your thoughts and put things in perspective. You'll also get a real buzz out of each other's company.

• *Saturday 3 January* •

If you want to get the best out of today you should rely on your innate ability to be flexible and versatile. If you can't do this for some reason, you'll feel edgy and out of sorts, because it looks like being one of those days when even the best-laid plans are likely to go up in smoke. There could also be a hiccup when someone with authority over you behaves very eccentrically.

• Sunday 4 January •

If possible, you should get together with friends today, especially if you haven't been able to see much of them during the recent festivities. There will be never a dull moment when you all meet up and you'll probably get jaw ache from all the talking that goes on. This is also a good day for losing yourself in a favourite hobby and forgetting about the rest of the world.

• Monday 5 January •

Once again, friends play a prominent role in your life, although today you'll be happiest with chums who share your spiritual views or cultural beliefs. You may even consider banding together in aid of a humanitarian or environmental cause, in which case you'll be able to combine your good intentions with your desire to make a difference to the world.

• Tuesday 6 January •

This is a super day for making a decision about a relationship, especially if you've been putting this off for some reason. Suddenly, you know exactly what you want to do and you're quite happy to nail your colours to the mast. Any decisions that you reach now will carry a lot of force and energy, so it's important that you don't rush into anything without thinking it through.

• *Wednesday 7 January* •

You're aware of a powerful bond uniting you with a certain person today. It seems to cross all sorts of barriers, such as physical distance, cultural differences and age gaps. Rather than concentrating on what separates you, you want to focus on what unites you. Be careful if you're experiencing this with someone who isn't your partner because you could fall for them now.

• *Thursday 8 January* •

Think twice before making any important financial moves because they could easily bring problems now. In fact, you'd be wise to postpone starting any new monetary activity today and instead to concentrate on projects that are already up and running. If you do start something, it's likely to get snarled up, fizzle out almost before it's begun, or bring you a heap of trouble.

• *Friday 9 January* •

Get out your party clothes and head for the nearest celebration today because you'll have a fantastic time. And if you don't have anything like this lined up, you'll have to improvise! You're in a marvellously optimistic and outgoing mood, which will dazzle everyone you meet. Just what you want if you're hoping to convince a certain someone that they can't live without you.

• *Saturday 10 January* •

In true Gemini fashion, you're extremely chatty today and will happily natter away to anyone who happens to be around. Mind you, everyone else is being equally voluble so you'll probably spend most of the day gassing your head off.

You could also collect some very interesting gossip but be wary about spreading it around too liberally unless you don't mind getting a reputation for being the local fount of all knowledge.

• *Sunday 11 January* •

Someone is being highly erratic and there's no way you'll be able to keep up with their rapid changes of mood. You may not even want to, because you'll probably find that a little of their company goes a long way right now. There could also be some domestic clashes over a loved one's need for independence, with other people wanting to clip their wings.

• *Monday 12 January* •

This is an excellent day for sorting out your current financial arrangements and making sure that everything is ticking over nicely. Try to unravel any problems now while the atmosphere is so harmonious and people are happy to help you. An in-depth conversation with someone dear to your heart will help to bring the two of you closer together.

• *Tuesday 13 January* •

The better you know someone, the more likely they are to get on your nerves today. They're saying things that get you gritting your teeth with irritation, and before you know it you'll be snapping at each other like a couple of grouchy terriers. Do your best to avoid dredging up past scores or throwing someone's previous transgressions back in their face, despite the temptation.

• *Wednesday 14 January* •

Between now and early February you should put on your thinking cap about your joint and official finances. It's a terrific opportunity to consider how you can make your money work for you, particularly if you can ask some experts for their opinions or do some research by yourself. Evaluate all your options carefully before finally making up your mind.

• *Thursday 15 January* •

If you've been telling yourself that you're immune to a certain person's charms, don't be too complacent today as you might suddenly feel as though you've been hit by a thunderbolt when you get a blast of their electrifying sex appeal. Where did all this come from and how long is it going to last? It's too early to tell but you must admit it's very exciting.

• *Friday 16 January* •

Fancy a trip around the shops? You're in the mood to do some nest-building and will really enjoy buying some objects to beautify your home. You don't have to spend a fortune in the process although that's certainly a possibility right now, since you'll have a tendency to get carried away. Make sure you can afford it before you start waving your credit card around.

• *Saturday 17 January* •

You're in an efficient and practical mood today and want to make sure that your life is running as smoothly as possible. So think about how you might achieve this. For instance, maybe you could make your working environment more pleasant, effective or ergonomic? You may also be inspired to make some sensible adjustments to your diet or health regime.

• *Sunday 18 January* •

It's very easy for someone to get carried away and make all sorts of promises that they can't deliver. It's unlikely that they're doing it deliberately or maliciously, so try not to think too badly of them when they fail to come up with the goods. You might also be rather irritated by their tendency to boast and blow their own trumpet at the moment.

• *Monday 19 January* •

Some of the people in your life are very lively today, and they'll do their best to get you involved in whatever has captured their imagination at the moment. As a result, a friend might ask you to come along to a new club that they've joined, or your partner could suggest that you both share in one of their favourite hobbies. You're in the mood to try anything right now!

• *Tuesday 20 January* •

A certain person is very persuasive today and they're keen that you do what they suggest. All will be well if you go along with their plans, but they won't be very pleased if you refuse to do as they ask. If that happens, they may give you the iron-hand-in-the-velvet-glove treatment and make it very obvious that they aren't pleased. But you won't want to give in to such pressure.

• *Wednesday 21 January* •

Opportunities will be knocking on your door fast and furious during the coming fortnight, so make sure you're ready to make the most of them. Some of these will announce themselves with a huge fanfare while others will require more discernment on your part. You'll also find that some of them fail to live up to expectations, but that others will be even better than you dared to hope.

• *Thursday 22 January* •

This is a good day to make some serious financial decisions, but you must be aware that you're tending to err on the side of caution right now. As a result, you'll feel reticent and anxious if you're being asked to overcommit yourself or take what you consider to be foolish risks. You must find a balance between being too wary and too reckless.

• *Friday 23 January* •

You can't bear the thought of any unnecessary restrictions or limitations being placed on you today, and you'll do your utmost to escape them. That's all very well if you're getting away from minor chores, but be careful if you get the urge to avoid important responsibilities because that could land you in hot water with the powers that be.

• *Saturday 24 January* •

If you're facing a difficult situation with someone, the best way to resolve it right now is to discuss it with them. This might seem rather daunting at first, especially if the current atmosphere between you isn't exactly convivial, but someone's got to make the first move and it might as well be you. Besides, think of how magnanimous and adult it will make you look. Not that you have any ulterior motives, of course. Perish the thought!

• *Sunday 25 January* •

Surround yourself with beloved faces and places today because they're exactly what you're in the mood for. Ideally, you should get together with some of your nearest and dearest, perhaps for a meal or just a chat. It will do your heart good to see them and you might also hatch some exciting schemes together.

• *Monday 26 January* •

Friends brighten up your life in many different ways today, whether they live round the corner or on the other side of the world. Get on the Internet and send them an e-mail, pick up the phone, or put pen to paper. The key message here is to communicate as much as possible, which shouldn't be too difficult for a lively Gemini like you.

• *Tuesday 27 January* •

Tread warily when talking to a certain person today because they seem to have temporarily lost their sense of humour. They're being rather po-faced and they're also more likely to point out your faults than rejoice in your good points. There could also be tension over someone's tendency to be possessive or their inability to share what they've got with you.

• *Wednesday 28 January* •

Turn your attention to your spare-time activities because one of them is about to grab you and fill you with enthusiasm. It might be something that you're already interested in but it's just as likely to be a pastime that you've never tried before, but which now grips you like a vice. You might also get very enthusiastic about a club or group that you've recently joined.

• *Thursday 29 January* •

This is a fantastic day because you've got the happy knack of getting on well with whoever happens to be around. But the most surprising aspect of today's events will be the way you effortlessly merge with someone who's supposed to be higher up the pecking order than you. You're getting on like a house on fire and it makes you feel great.

• *Friday 30 January* •

Someone is in the mood to confide in you today, so make sure that you treat their confidences with consideration and respect. Not that you should have any problems with this because you're in a very thoughtful mood. If you're attracted to someone who's in a position of power, you'll be even more tantalized by what happens between you now.

• *Saturday 31 January* •

This is a fantastic day to take part in any sort of discussion or negotiation because you're so keen to ensure that everyone gets a fair deal and no one loses out. This may mean that you decide not to take unfair advantage over someone, and you'll soon realize that this is exactly the right approach to take. It will prove how honourable your intentions are.

FEBRUARY AT A GLANCE

Love	❤ ❤ ❤
Money	£ $ £
Career	💻 💻 💻 💻 💻
Health	☼ ☼

• *Sunday 1 February* •

You're in a very adventurous mood today and are keen to push back the boundaries of your life in some way. You won't want to do anything too radical or outrageous, but you'll certainly get a big kick out of setting yourself a challenge and then seeing how you meet it. Thoughts of travel are whirling around your head, too, so how about organizing a forthcoming trip or holiday?

• *Monday 2 February* •

This is a great day for emphasizing the spiritual and religious aspects of your life. You want to merge with something bigger than yourself, whatever that happens to be. What takes place as a result will be life-enhancing and profound, but you'll have to resist the temptation to turn it into something bigger than it really is.

• *Tuesday 3 February* •

Between now and late March you won't have as much motivation and energy as usual, and what you do have will be difficult to channel in the right directions. As a result, there will be times when you feel you're frittering away your energy and not getting anywhere. You may also be reluctant to stand up for yourself when others are trying to get at you, but it's important that you do so if you don't want to set a precedent for the future.

• *Wednesday 4 February* •

This is a good day for taking care of your domestic needs and making sure that everyone at home is happy and content. This will be easier than you might imagine because it seems that the rest of the family are doing their best to be cheerful and positive. If you're going shopping it's a good idea to take someone along to keep you company and help you carry all those bags.

• *Thursday 5 February* •

Keep a grip on your temper today because you'll have a tendency to get worked up over the slightest little thing. Once that happens, you could bite people's heads off and, in the process, say something that really upsets them. So be careful about wading in with both feet and do your best to monitor your thoughts before you blurt them out in the heat of the moment.

• *Friday 6 February* •

You're a creature of ideas who excels at communicating with others, but over the next two weeks you'll have to do some serious thinking about some of the ways in which you connect with the people around you. For instance, you might realize that you have a tendency to dominate the conversation or that you're quite opinionated, making you want to moderate this behaviour.

• *Saturday 7 February* •

Your mind is eager for some exercise from today and during the next three weeks it will take you on some fabulous journeys. Try not to put any limitations on your thoughts or ideas, and instead allow yourself to be swept along by the current of your enthusiasm. You might even be inspired to enrol in a college course or evening class.

• *Sunday 8 February* •

Friends will play an important role in your life between now and early February, giving you the opportunity to get even closer to some of them. There's also a chance that what started out as a platonic relationship will develop into something romantic and loving now, much to your delight. However, try not to idealize this person out of all recognition.

• *Monday 9 February* •

Be wary about getting drawn into discussions about politics, religion, ecology or anything else that's likely to raise someone's hackles. It's the sort of day when an innocent conversation quickly escalates into a right old ding-dong, with everyone eager to score points or make sly digs. If this happens you could easily be tempted to say more than you intended, with sticky results.

• Tuesday 10 February •

You're in a very affectionate and loving mood today, making you eager to get on well with whoever happens to stray across your path. You'll do your best to treat them with consideration and respect, even if you don't agree with their views or have other reasons for not liking them very much. If you've got the time you'll enjoy a visit to an art gallery or museum.

• Wednesday 11 February •

You're at your most outgoing and gregarious today, so it's a wonderful day for mixing with some of your favourite people. If you're going to a party or celebration you'll quickly become one of the focal points of the room, and are quite likely to make a new friend in the process. If you play your cards right, you might even meet someone who will become a lover in the future.

• Thursday 12 February •

You need all your patience today, otherwise colleagues and customers will push you to the limit. You're trying to cram too much activity into too short a time frame, and as a result you're feeling pressured, tense and ratty. Do you really have to work at this breakneck speed, or are you trying to prove a point to someone who's a bit of a slowcoach?

• *Friday 13 February* •

If things were tense yesterday they're even more frazzled today. It looks as though a storm is gathering, in which case it would be much better to get it out of the way sooner rather than later. Stick to the salient facts and don't let yourself get worked up into such a lather that you damage your relationship with someone or sound like a ranting, small-minded idiot.

• *Saturday 14 February* •

If you had high hopes of what Valentine's Day would bring, it looks as though you're going to have to revise your expectations rather drastically. Maybe the object of your affections is unavoidably busy elsewhere, or they're with you in body but not in spirit. Don't panic unless this is par for the course and further evidence that you're growing apart.

• *Sunday 15 February* •

Open your mind to a whole host of possibilities today, especially if you would normally dismiss them as being fanciful or just plain daft. For instance, you might now become interested in ghosts, astrology, tarot or anything else that delves into the mysterious side of life. Mystical topics will also appeal and set you thinking, so be receptive to all sorts of ideas now.

• *Monday 16 February* •

Financial worries are nagging away at you, putting a crimp in your day and making you feel rather wretched. The first thing to do is to work out whether you're justified in feeling this way or whether you're worrying over nothing. The second is to decide what you're going to do about it. You won't get anywhere if you just dither and chew your fingernails. So take action!

• *Tuesday 17 February* •

If you're currently planning some domestic improvements or are thinking about moving house, today is a good day to grab a pen and paper and do some sums. It's important that you work out a budget and right now you're in a very money-minded mood. You're also feeling quite positive, but beware of being too optimistic and, as a result, becoming unrealistic.

• *Wednesday 18 February* •

Snap, snap, snap! A certain person is like a crocodile today as they prowl around, showing their teeth and growling. They're in the sort of mood in which it's impossible to reason with them and you may decide that your best bet is to put as much distance between you as possible until they've calmed down and started to behave themselves again.

• *Thursday 19 February* •

Over the next four weeks you'd be wise to concentrate as much as possible on your career and long-term goals. These will be highlighted, fuelling your ambitions and making you eager to boost your reputation in some way. If you've been slogging away for ages now with little or no recognition, it seems that your ship is finally going to come in. Yippee!

• *Friday 20 February* •

You're a skilled conversationalist today and will enjoy putting across your point of view. You're also in quite an analytical mood so you'll enjoy questioning people and getting to the nub of what they're saying. If there has been a mystery lately between you and a partner, today is a good opportunity to get to the bottom of it and set your mind at rest.

• *Saturday 21 February* •

Hmmm, someone is drunk on power today. They're throwing their weight around and acting as though they're the only person on the planet, or so it seems to you. The question is whether you're being too sensitive about this or whether you're dead right. Either way, think twice before challenging them because you risk being drawn into an uncomfortable battle of wills.

• *Sunday 22 February* •

You have a strong need to assert your independence and free will today, and you'll hate the thought or being tied down or restricted in any way. However, it's highly likely that you are being limited, perhaps by what's expected of you right now or simply by society's morals. It's up to you how much you kick against this but bear in mind that embracing the role of the revolutionary or outsider could come at a high price. Are you willing to pay it?

• *Monday 23 February* •

Trust your instincts and intuition today and you won't go far wrong. Right now you're able to tune in to the unspoken messages that people are sending you, and also to filter out anything that's a distraction. Take advantage of this by establishing a more compassionate and empathic link with friends and the other people you meet now.

• *Tuesday 24 February* •

Strange goings-on are affecting you right now, with some peculiar events taking place. You may be completely unable to explain them, yet you know they're real. For instance, you might have a striking experience of ESP or telepathy. You may also suspect that a certain person is trying to trip you up or hinder you in some way, so you should be very wary of them until you've got a better idea of what they're up to.

• Wednesday 25 February •

It's time to turn your thoughts towards your aims and ambitions, and to think hard about what you want to achieve in 2004. Don't underestimate yourself or your abilities, because it looks as though you could go far. It may help to discuss your plans with someone who can point you in the right direction or give you plenty of encouragement.

• Thursday 26 February •

You're blessed with boundless energy and enthusiasm this Thursday, which is great for getting things done. You're especially keen to get busy around your home or garden, but it's important to pace yourself and know your limitations; otherwise you might bite off a lot more than you can chew. You could also run out of steam halfway through a job and then really struggle to complete it.

• Friday 27 February •

It's great fun to say things that raise eyebrows and ruffle feathers today, but it's important that you know when to stop. If you don't, you run the risk of provoking a lot of bad feeling and getting yourself labelled as a troublemaker. You should be especially careful when dealing with people in authority, because they won't approve of your actions and may even want to come down on you like a ton of bricks. So rebel in modest ways!

• *Saturday 28 February* •

You're capable of achieving a tremendous amount today if you're prepared to put your head down and work hard. However, other considerations such as your personal life will have to go by the wayside for the time being. If this is going to cause ructions with certain people, try to explain what's going on to them and ask them for their understanding and tolerance.

• *Sunday 29 February* •

You've certainly got your head screwed on the right way today, especially when it comes to thinking along financial and business lines. You know exactly what's what and you want to be as efficient as possible. If you've got to negotiate a deal or ask for a pay rise in the next few days, this is your chance to map out your strategy and possibly even draft what you're going to say. Right now it's unlikely that you'll put a foot wrong.

MARCH AT A GLANCE

Love	♥ ♥
Money	£ $
Career	💻 💻 💻 💻 💻
Health	☼ ☼

• *Monday 1 March* •

If this is the start of your working week you'll want to give it your best shot and be as effective as possible. This shouldn't be hard, given your current state of mind. Don't lose sight of your ultimate goals, Gemini, even if your progress towards them seems to be really slow right now. Remember the story about the tortoise and the hare, and then keep plodding on. You'll get there in the end! In the meantime, enjoy the journey.

• *Tuesday 2 March* •

It's a day for shopping, whether you're spending big bucks or simply picking up a few items for the store cupboard. It will give you a lovely warm feeling to buy articles that will add to the comfort or appearance of your home. You could easily be tempted to splash out on a couple of bottles of wine or a delicious pudding, especially if you'd promised yourself that you'd leave such things on the shop shelves. Farewell, will-power, hallo, chocolate!

• *Wednesday 3 March* •

There's a wonderfully intense atmosphere between you and a special person today. Although you aren't always comfortable about expressing your innermost emotions in case that leaves you in a vulnerable position, right now you're prepared to let your guard down a little because of the benefits you'll get in return. So open your heart to someone, even if it's in an entirely platonic way.

• *Thursday 4 March* •

Someone has big ideas today and they aren't afraid to share them with anyone who'll listen. Your inbuilt censor will be asking whether these plans are realistic or simply pie in the sky. But before telling this person that they're talking a lot of hogwash, perhaps you should listen more carefully because there could be some elements of genius in what they're saying.

• *Friday 5 March* •

If it's been a case of eyes across a crowded room, coded conversations and restless nights wondering whether you-know-who is as nuts about you as you are about them, then prepare for the emotional rollercoaster that lies ahead. You'll delight in being as romantic as possible, and if some subterfuge is involved that will only add some delicious spice to the situation.

• *Saturday 6 March* •

Today's Full Moon is urging you to take constructive action about the domestic tensions that are currently bugging you. Now, although it's tempting to tell yourself that these are all the fault of other people and you're the innocent party, deep down you know that it isn't quite that simple. So think about how you've contributed to the situation and how you can now make amends.

• *Sunday 7 March* •

Despite yesterday's high-minded resolutions, you haven't yet managed to sort out the tricky atmosphere affecting your home and family, as today's events prove only too well. It will be the easiest thing in the world to get drawn into a right old ding-dong with someone in which you hurl insults back and forth, but what is that going to achieve in the long run? A big fat nothing.

• *Monday 8 March* •

Your thoughts turn inward today, putting you in an introspective mood. This is just what you need if you want to examine your motives and desires in a lot of detail. However, try not to get caught up in a mental loop in which you go round and round in circles without achieving anything. You should also avoid rehashing past resentments and planning your revenge. Not the answer!

• *Tuesday 9 March* •

There are some very interesting developments in your relationship with a certain person today, especially if you're trying to pretend to the outside world that nothing's going on. The sexual energy between you is in danger of reaching fever pitch, so what are you going to do about it? You're both in the mood to take some risks but don't push your luck.

• *Wednesday 10 March* •

This is a fantastic day for putting your head down and getting on with whatever work is waiting for you. You're feeling businesslike and efficient, and you'll also manage to concentrate on what you're doing without being distracted by stray thoughts. You may have to make a decision about the cost of a health treatment or a work expense.

• *Thursday 11 March* •

Once again you're keen to get on with whichever tasks are on the agenda. Things will go very smoothly because not only are you at your most effective right now but you also have the happy knack of being able to work well with the people around you. It's a great day if you're involved in some form of team work because it will be seamless right now.

• *Friday 12 March* •

Prepare for a battle of wills today, with a conflict between someone's desire for change and another person's need for things to stay the same. If you're involved in this, you'll quickly reach stalemate because it seems that no one is prepared to give an inch and they want to have things all their own way. You're going to have to wait for a more favourable time before pursuing this.

• *Saturday 13 March* •

Life feels pretty tense right now, so prepare for a few fireworks today. If you're still brooding about what happened yesterday, or feeling angry with someone because of their intransigence, it's highly likely that you'll lose your temper before too long. But be careful about who you yell at – don't antagonize anyone who's in a position of power over you and who could make life difficult.

• *Sunday 14 March* •

Do a little lateral thinking today – it will help you to solve problems that have stumped you until now. Don't be shy about stretching your mind in new directions and seeing what comes up as a result. You could also be offered the chance to make some clever moves in a financial transaction or investment, but keep your feet on the ground over this.

• *Monday 15 March* •

Behind that smiling exterior lurks someone who is no stranger to worry, and today it's got you firmly in its grip. It will be very difficult to shut off from these anxieties but the more you think about them, the worse they'll seem. Before you know where you are, you'll have got yourself into a total panic unless you can be very strict with yourself. Do your best!

• *Tuesday 16 March* •

If you need some expert advice, this is the day to get it. People are being very co-operative and friendly, encouraging you to ask them whatever is uppermost in your mind. Make the most of this amenable atmosphere because it will help you to clear up all sorts of minor problems and red tape that have been bothering you lately.

• *Wednesday 17 March* •

Do yourself a favour and make plenty of time for enjoyment today. It's exactly what you're in the mood for and you'll feel that you're missing out if you can't let your hair down at some point. Ideally, you should get together with people who you feel completely comfortable with, such as close family or friends. Open a bottle, share some food and enjoy one another's company.

• *Thursday 18 March* •

If something has been bugging you lately you're now determined to fix it so that you can concentrate on other things instead. This may involve a certain amount of guts or energy, but you have plenty of both right now. You may even have to tell someone a few home truths but you'll do this in a very measured way to avoid rubbing them up the wrong way.

• *Friday 19 March* •

Be careful today because it will be awfully easy to fall into an egocentric trap. Your instincts are telling you to help others and to explore the spiritual side of life, and one way in which you might do this is to get involved with a good cause or to talk about your personal beliefs. Great, but don't let this go to your head and make you feel as though you're something special or a martyr.

• *Saturday 20 March* •

There's a massive planetary emphasis on your friendships from today, and during the coming month you'll certainly benefit if you can concentrate on this side of life. Not only will you enjoy being with chums, you could also make new contacts who will help you in the future. A cherished wish will get a new lease of life now, but are you prepared to follow it through to a conclusion?

• *Sunday 21 March* •

How are you feeling? From today you'll start to become a lot more energetic and dynamic than you've been in ages, and you'll be looking for directions in which to channel all this power and vitality. It's a great time to concentrate on personal projects and also to take the initiative, but watch out for a possible tendency to think that you're the only pebble on the beach right now.

• *Monday 22 March* •

If there has been a slight misunderstanding with someone lately, make an effort to talk about it and work your way through it today. Be prepared to examine your feelings with honesty, and to tell this person how you're feeling. However, you may have to modify some things in order not to hurt them unnecessarily.

• *Tuesday 23 March* •

If you feel trapped by a certain person's expectations or opinion of you because it seems to be at such odds with the way you really are, you'll get the chance to do something about it now. You might be able to drop a few hints into the conversation or do something that shows you don't fit into the neat little pigeon-hole they've made for you.

• *Wednesday 24 March* •

You're naturally inquisitive at the best of times and you're even more curious about the world today. You aren't prepared to accept things at face value because you want to find out more about them. It's a wonderful day for having in-depth conversations with friends and partners, and you could talk about some very serious topics that definitely need airing.

• *Thursday 25 March* •

You're in a bit of a hurry today, aren't you? There's a lot you want to achieve and you won't be very happy if you feel you're being restricted or slowed down by others. However, try to guard against the tendency to do things so quickly that you muck them up or make silly mistakes. You also need to burn off excess nervous energy to prevent it turning into irritation with others.

• *Friday 26 March* •

Do some socializing today, especially if you're getting together with friends and other kindred spirits. You'll all hit it off and you might even make some new chums in the course of the day. If you're still feeling your way with a new acquaintance, make an effort to break the ice with them now and the atmosphere between you will become warmer and more intimate.

• *Saturday 27 March* •

Relationships could be slightly fraught today, thanks to the way someone is taking everything so seriously. They may also be on some sort of power trip, so you feel that they're bossing you about or giving you the message that you should be subservient to them. Unless it's vital that you say something it will probably be better for you to step back from the situation and let it blow over.

• *Sunday 28 March* •

Freedom! Liberation! These are really important ideas for you today and you'll get extremely angry if you're denied them. You'll also want to rebel against anyone or anything that seems to be clipping your wings and if you aren't careful you'll spend the entire day fired up with revolutionary fury. If you're constructive and creative about this you'll make some positive changes, but don't use it as an excuse to wreak havoc and cause trouble.

• *Monday 29 March* •

You're in a much more gentle mood than you were yesterday and want to enjoy your home comforts in peace and quiet. So make the place as cosy and relaxing as possible, and then revel in it. It's a good day for being creative in the kitchen and you'll enjoy cooking some of your favourite meals.

• *Tuesday 30 March* •

Think twice before mixing business with pleasure because they're likely to clash right now. Someone might speak out of turn or there could be problems about what is expected of you. If you're thinking about buying something involved in a favourite hobby, there could be a problem over the cost of it, raising questions about how much you're prepared to spend on enjoyment.

• *Wednesday 31 March* •

Your social life more than lives up to expectations today, so it would be a shame to spend too much time by yourself.

Arrange to see some friends if you don't have anything planned, or invite a neighbour in for a drink. You'll enjoy getting involved in conversations that set you thinking and allow you to show off your dazzling thought processes. You're at your quick-witted best right now.

APRIL AT A GLANCE

Love	♥ ♥ ♥ ♥
Money	£ $
Career	💻 💻
Health	☼ ☼ ☼

● Thursday 1 April ●

You aren't usually tongue-tied but that's the way you'll feel during the next couple of weeks. You'll be reluctant to speak up when necessary and will also be much keener than normal to keep your thoughts a secret than to broadcast them to everyone. Do your best not to give the impression that you're being sneaky or manipulative and, if necessary, explain that you simply don't feel much like talking at the moment.

● Friday 2 April ●

You have a strong hankering to be with close family and other loved ones today, particularly if you can fuss over them and look after them. You might also be gripped by some sentimental feelings that aren't your usual style but which need to expressed. Nostalgia is also not far away now and you might have a happy time looking through old photos or mementos.

• *Saturday 3 April* •

Take a look in the mirror and decide honestly whether your image is due for an update. You don't have to overhaul yourself from top to toe, especially if you can't afford it, but your confidence will receive a life-enhancing boost if you can devote more time to your appearance. Get your hair done, buy the most flattering cosmetics you can find or treat yourself to some new clothes, and then bask in the compliments that will come your way.

• *Sunday 4 April* •

The more you're prepared to accept people on their own terms and dismiss any unrealistic expectations of them, the closer you'll get to them today. Play your cards right and you might even forge some strong links with someone who will teach you a great deal about the spiritual or religious side of life. You'll also get a lot out of a church ceremony or some other form of ritual now.

• *Monday 5 April* •

Your ideas about a loved one will be called into question during the coming two weeks. This doesn't have to be an alarming or negative experience because you might realize that this person is becoming increasingly important to you and that you've got to devote more time to them in the future. If there are problems with someone, work through them together now.

• *Tuesday 6 April* •

Communications start to get snarled up from today and unfortunately they won't sort themselves out until the end of the month. This means that you'll have to be very careful about what you say and don't say, bearing in mind that your silence will be a lot more eloquent than any amount of words. Beware of sending out confusing or misleading messages.

• *Wednesday 7 April* •

If you're currently on the hunt for a new home or want to renovate your existing place, you could have a mini stroke of luck today. For instance, someone might pass on the name of the perfect builder or decorator, or you might spot a property that's got your name on it. If you're out shopping for domestic items you could find some real bargains.

• *Thursday 8 April* •

It's good to get close to a certain person today but you won't like it if they become too demanding. However, is this fair? You may be sending them the message, loud and clear, that you want to be with them, and then sending them another message saying that you've had enough of them for the time being, thank you very much. No wonder they're feeling upset!

• *Friday 9 April* •

Someone wants to be a free spirit today and they won't like it if they feel their wings are being clipped. Does this sound like you? If so, you must guard against the tendency to bite the hand that feeds you by rejecting the very people you depend upon, simply because they're making demands on you or you have a very low boredom threshold at the moment. Take it easy! Let off steam by doing something exciting but don't hurt others in the process.

• *Saturday 10 April* •

Relationships are causing you slight problems at the moment and unfortunately this is another day when certain people are likely to get on your wick. This time, you're feeling suffocated by the intensity of a certain person and their complete inability to leave you alone, whether mentally, physically or emotionally. What do they want from you, blood? Make your excuses and put some distance between you before you start to scream.

• *Sunday 11 April* •

The more receptive you are to change, the more you'll get out of what happens today. This is one of those times in your life when you can make great personal progress if you're prepared to acknowledge what needs to be done and to move forward. Although relationships are one of the areas that will be most affected, you also need to think about how you can transform your dreams into reality.

• *Monday 12 April* •

There's no doubt about it – someone is being utterly unreasonable today. Well, that's the way it seems to you although they're bound to tell a different story. And this is the key to handling today's problems, because you must take responsibility for your part in what happens and also do your utmost to find a solution that suits everyone concerned and not just you. Not easy, but worth it.

• *Tuesday 13 April* •

From today until the end of the month it won't always be easy to communicate well with friends. You might find that you keep saying the wrong thing, or there could be problems involved in getting in touch with them for the time being. Do your best to smooth over any problems as soon as they crop up to avoid them assuming too much importance in anyone's mind.

• *Wednesday 14 April* •

You're ready to throw open your doors and play the host or hostess with the mostest today. The thought of doing some entertaining, whether it's modest or totally over the top, is almost too good to resist. However, it will be far better to know your limits and have a massive success than to overstretch yourself and end up doing everything in a rather mediocre manner.

• *Thursday 15 April* •

You could find yourself in the limelight today, especially if you're being congratulated for your talents and abilities. Enjoy it while it lasts! You'll also benefit from the patronage of someone older or more influential than you, and who has your best interests at heart. They may do you a favour or pull some strings on your behalf.

• *Friday 16 April* •

You won't like it one bit if you suspect that someone is trying to get the upper hand today. In fact, you'll make your displeasure very plain, which could lead to some tricky moments. Be very careful about the way you're behaving because your actions and facial expressions will be far more eloquent and revealing than you know. If you don't like what someone is saying or doing, you'll show it through subtle but powerful gestures.

• *Saturday 17 April* •

A friend is in a very garrulous mood and it will be difficult to shut them up for long. Not that you'll want to, because you'll enjoy having a good old natter with them. However, if they fail to let you get a word in edgeways you'll soon feel hard-done-by and will manage to slip in a few caustic comments. If you're ringing someone up you might spend ages talking, so consider your phone bill!

• *Sunday 18 April* •

Make the most of your spare time today by getting busy with a favourite hobby or pastime. Ideally, this should involve a certain amount of energy and get you out of the house. You'll enjoy being in the fresh air, returning home pleasantly tired and hungry. A friend will try to talk you into doing something with them and you won't need much urging.

• *Monday 19 April* •

Today's eclipsed New Moon will have an invigorating effect on your friendships during the rest of the month. You might realize that you've got to turn over a new leaf with someone if you want your relationship to continue, or you may decide that you must give them a second chance. This is also a great time to join a club or organization that will introduce you to some new faces.

• *Tuesday 20 April* •

Someone is abundantly kind and considerate towards you today, much to your delight. For a start, they'll cheer you up and make you laugh. But they may also tuck you under their wing or look out for you in some way. If you're in the midst of some home improvement plans, this is a good day to pat everyone on the back for all their recent efforts and give them some encouragement.

• *Wednesday 21 April* •

You're really only interested in finding the best in other people today, making you fully prepared to overlook all their little foibles and faults. What's more, you hope they'll do the same for you. However, you must revert to a more realistic attitude soon or you'll be in danger of allowing someone to trick you, or of deceiving yourself about someone's integrity or intentions.

• *Thursday 22 April* •

Watch out because it's one of those rather uncomfortable days in which you're battling against what you believe to be restrictions and curbs. For instance, you may want to go out and play but instead you've got to stay chained to your desk while slogging through a great pile of work. You might also be outraged by the pettifogging bureaucracy that's being inflicted on you.

• *Friday 23 April* •

You're dashing around like a mad thing today, desperately trying to find enough hours in the day for everything you want to achieve. Well, unfortunately you'll end up going round in ever-decreasing circles unless you can channel your energy in constructive directions and not waste it on getting impatient with people who are operating at a slower pace.

• *Saturday 24 April* •

Be extremely careful when dealing with other people today, especially if you're on a collision course as a result of a disagreement or battle of wills. Neither of you will be willing to back down, although you'll fully expect the other person to capitulate. This won't achieve anything worthwhile, and will doubtless end in some very hard feelings and some powerful enmity. It's simply not worth the hassle!

• *Sunday 25 April* •

You're in a much more amenable mood today, so grab the chance to talk about what went wrong yesterday and try to put matters right. Both of you must be prepared to discuss what happened, so encourage the other person to be open by behaving in that way yourself. Setting a good example will have a strong impact on everyone around you, so don't underestimate its effects.

• *Monday 26 April* •

If you're arranging a forthcoming social event, this is a good day to get on with all the organization involved. It's an especially good day for checking facts, getting prices for things and generally keeping everyone informed. In some cases, you may have to spell things out in great detail in order to avoid getting your wires crossed and ending up in a total muddle. So be clear and eloquent.

• *Tuesday 27 April* •

Go gently when talking to neighbours and other people you see on a regular basis, because your idea of a joke and theirs don't match right now. So you might make what you think is a witty wisecrack, only to watch it sink like a stone. Even worse, you could be ticked off for not taking something seriously enough. Is this true, or are they suffering from a sense of humour failure?

• *Wednesday 28 April* •

No matter how well or badly things are going in your life at the moment, you can't help feeling positive and upbeat today. It's a great opportunity to count your blessings, although you'll think of so many that you'll soon run out of fingers and toes.

There could be great news about a family or property matter, and you'll also enjoy being with your nearest and dearest. A great day!

• *Thursday 29 April* •

The more defensive or reticent someone is today the more you'll want to shake them. However, that wouldn't be a good idea. Besides, it seems that you've both adopted entrenched positions right now and you're at such odds that you'll really struggle to find any sort of compromise at all. Resist the temptation to do something that will really shock or alarm this person.

• *Friday 30 April* •

At long last, after a month in which communications were all over the place, you're beginning to feel more confident about getting your message across in the spirit in which it was meant. But don't expect every tricky situation to solve itself like magic. You may still have to pour oil on troubled waters and mollify certain people, but that will be a small price to pay for the peace and quiet that ensues.

MAY AT A GLANCE

Love	♥ ♥ ♥ ♥ ♥
Money	£ $ £ $
Career	💻 💻 💻 💻 💻
Health	☼ ☼ ☼ ☼ ☼

• *Saturday 1 May* •

This is a terrific day for making long-term decisions about your finances and domestic arrangements, especially if you want to make some improvements to these areas of your life. You'll manage to blend caution where necessary with optimism when it's appropriate, so you'll get the very best possible combination for your current situation. Use this time well.

• Sunday 2 May •

Last month you faced some powerful tussles with certain people, in which neither of you was prepared to back down one iota. Unfortunately, it looks as though you're confronted by another round of this today, and the stakes seem just as high as they were in April. How long do you think you can keep this up? Or do you think it's time to capitulate and call a truce?

• Monday 3 May •

Love has a fabulous effect on you today so make every effort to get together with loved ones at every opportunity. Ideally, you should go out on the town, visit the cinema or go out for a meal together. Or maybe you'd rather stay at home and disappear into a romantic world of your own with you-know-who? Whatever you do, you'll enjoy it.

• Tuesday 4 May •

Today's eclipsed Full Moon is reminding you that you can't take your health for granted. If it's been ages since you last had a check-up at the dentist's or doctor's, get on the phone now and arrange something. Not very exciting, admittedly, but it's important that you take good care of yourself. A healthy dietary regime might also be on the cards now.

• Wednesday 5 May •

To hear a certain person talk, you'd think they were the Dalai Lama and Mother Theresa rolled into one. They're busy giving you the impression that they're in line for sainthood and almost too good to be true. Now, before you swallow this whole, ask yourself why they're telling you all this. What are they trying to prove? They may be trying to sting you in some way.

• *Thursday 6 May* •

You're full of consideration towards others today and will want to do what you can to make their lives more easy. However, you won't want to make a big song and dance about this by advertising your good intentions, nor will you want to rob anyone of their dignity. Instead, you'll want to do what you can in as modest and unassuming a way as possible. Good for you!

• *Friday 7 May* •

Between now and late June you'll want to devote a lot of energy to your priorities and values, and you'll defend them tooth and nail if you have to. Try not to let things get out of proportion, however, so that you become defensive and huffy if anyone questions where your loyalties lie. This will also be a good time to take part in financial negotiations because you'll be formidable.

• *Saturday 8 May* •

It's one of those days when your thoughts will quickly spiral out of control unless you can exercise enough discipline to keep them in order. You're also showing a tendency to imagine that things are much worse than they really are, so if any bills arrive you'll immediately go into a panic and wonder how you're going to pay them even if you've got plenty of money. Calm down!

• *Sunday 9 May* •

This is a fantastic day for telling close partners how you feel, and encouraging them to do the same with you. Much to your surprise, you may even find yourselves talking about topics that are usually off limits or too sensitive to mention. It will be a relief to get these out into the open and to find out how you all feel about them. So don't clam up through shyness or embarrassment.

• *Monday 10 May* •

Try to devote as much time as possible to friends now because you'll derive real pleasure from their company. It will be even better if you're having a reunion with someone you haven't seen for a while, because you'll have a fabulous time together. You aren't always very good at being demonstrative and affectionate, Gemini, but give your chums a big hug today.

• *Tuesday 11 May* •

If you're trying to keep a secret you'd better take a vow of silence today, otherwise you're horribly likely to blurt out everything by accident. What's more, the more you tell yourself that you mustn't say something, the longer it will be on the tip of your tongue. Change the subject or make yourself scarce. Anything is better than talking about what is supposed to be confidential.

• *Wednesday 12 May* •

The merest hint of red tape has you foaming at the mouth today, so be careful when faced by rules and regulations. If you're asked to fill in a form, your first instinct will be to tear it up into little pieces and jump up and down on them, but that won't do you any favours and might even mean that a beady-eyed official will have you in their sights. Not a wise move, you must agree.

• Thursday 13 May •

There's a lot you can achieve today but you'll be at your most effective if you're left to work at your own pace, without interruptions from anyone else. It's not that you're feeling unfriendly, simply that you're quite happy to be left to your own devices for the time being. And with certain people behaving as they are right now, it's a blessed relief to be allowed to do your own thing.

• Friday 14 May •

Life should be quite easy today, although you'll have to cope with a woman who gets a bit agitated and het up. It won't take much to calm her down, and probably the best way to do this is to give her as much attention as possible. She's after her share of the limelight and she'll cause trouble until she gets it. So smile at her, talk to her, and make her feel noticed.

• Saturday 15 May •

Unfortunately it looks as though you're going to be disappointed about something today. A financial arrangement might hit the skids or meet delays, forcing you to be patient until things are up and running again. It's not a good idea to boast about any of your material benefits, whether large or small, in case someone tries to put you down or make you feel guilty about them.

• Sunday 16 May •

During the next few weeks you'll really relish having some time for reflection, especially if you can be left alone while you're musing on life. You might even become interested in some form of meditation or prayer during this phase, or want to increase the amount of time you already spend on such activities. It's also a good opportunity to keep a journal of your thoughts.

• *Monday 17 May* •

From today until the end of June, events will encourage you to examine the way you connect with the other people in your life. Of course, none of us can get it right all the time but you need to consider which areas of your relationships need the most work. Are you too dependent on others? Too critical of them? Too eager to please? Come on, be honest about this and, in doing so, become more aware of your own behaviour.

• *Tuesday 18 May* •

You can't help thinking that a certain person would lose their head if it wasn't screwed on, and they're giving vivid examples of this right now. They're being very absent-minded and distracted, so you're lucky if you can get much sense out of them. It's no good getting annoyed with them because that will only make them more flustered and daffy. You'll have to grin and bear it.

• *Wednesday 19 May* •

Today's New Moon is suggesting that you look deeply into the most private and hidden recesses of your life, and examine what you find there. The more scary this prospect sounds, the more you stand to benefit from it because it will enable you to look difficult facts in the face and possibly even get something productive out of them. For instance, if you had a difficult childhood you might decide to give your support to a children's charity, so that others don't have to suffer in the way that you did.

• *Thursday 20 May* •

Over the next four weeks you'll want to devote a lot of time and energy to personal projects, and will be far more interested in your own concerns than in those of other people. This is entirely natural right now although you may have to disguise your self-interest every now and then in order to avoid seeming totally egocentric and selfish.

• *Friday 21 May* •

You're in an inventive frame of mind today and you'll come up with some brilliant ideas. Try not to keep these to yourself because you'll really excel if you're taking part in some sort of think tank or group brainstorming session. Some of what you say may sound futuristic or avant-garde to less far-seeing souls but that doesn't mean you should curb your thinking or keep quiet.

• *Saturday 22 May* •

Be careful when spending money because it will slip through your fingers like sand. You'll enjoy every minute of it, of course, although it will be a different story when the credit card or bank statements land on the mat. If you're buying domestic items you'll find it horribly easy to talk yourself into getting all sorts of things that you don't really need but simply can't resist.

• *Sunday 23 May* •

Think twice before making any major purchase or investment today because it could all end in tears or nothing will come of it. It will also be a headache to unravel all the problems that will develop further down the line. So hold fire until tomorrow if possible, which will give you the chance to mull over whether you're doing the right thing and still want to go ahead with it.

• *Monday 24 May* •

You're at the centre of a social whirl today, which will be utterly delightful and will do your ego no end of good. It's an especially good day for mixing with close relatives and neighbours, and just generally enjoying one another's company. You might also be asked to take part in a local event, such as a forthcoming fête or show.

• *Tuesday 25 May* •

Concentrate on your finances today but don't expect everything to run like clockwork. You could encounter delays or other frustrating blocks to your progress. If things get really bogged down you'll have to consider whether you're asking the impossible right now or whether you're being perfectly reasonable and it's others who are being difficult.

• *Wednesday 26 May* •

This is a fantastic day for talking about whatever is uppermost in your mind. You're in the mood to get things off your chest, but without causing ructions or ill feeling. Instead, you'll manage to keep people sweet and not tread on any toes, while still describing your feelings. This will be quite a feat and it's not one to be sniffed at, so make the most of this silver-tongued phase while it lasts.

• *Thursday 27 May* •

You have a strong urge to kick against the traces today, but you must be really careful how you do this. Although you'd dearly love to thumb your nose at authority in some way, this will simply put you on a crash course with people who are determined to make you play the game. Be especially wary about annoying officials, bureaucrats and powerbrokers at the moment.

• *Friday 28 May* •

It's a strange day and you aren't entirely sure of what's going on around you. That's because certain people are being sneaky, manipulative and untrustworthy. They may also be saying what they think you want to hear in an effort to twist you round their little finger. Watch out, too, for anyone who's being holier-than-thou in order to make themselves feel good.

• *Saturday 29 May* •

It would be a shame if you had to spend the whole day by yourself because you've got so much to give other people right now, such as warmth, love and laughter. If you're currently a solo Gemini then you might not be that way for much longer as there's a strong chance that you'll fall in love with someone you meet now. And they'll be smitten with you, too. Yes!

• *Sunday 30 May* •

Surround yourself with beauty today. No, that doesn't mean endlessly looking in the mirror! Visit a lovely stretch of countryside or seashore, stroll around an art gallery or lie in the garden soaking up the sun. This is a day for retreating from your cares and worries and feeding your soul by doing things that remind you how simple and perfect life can be.

• *Monday 31 May* •

You're full of optimism today, which is great for plodding on with projects that haven't gone very well lately. However, there's a chance that you could come across as arrogant, patronizing or complacent, especially if you're feeling rather pleased with yourself. A little modesty wouldn't go amiss now. You must also guard against taking on more than you can manage in a domestic project.

JUNE AT A GLANCE

Love	♥ ♥ ♥ ♥ ♥
Money	£ $ £ $ £
Career	💻 💻 💻 💻 💻
Health	☼ ☼ ☼ ☼ ☼

● Tuesday 1 June ●

You've got so many things buzzing around inside your head that it's virtually impossible to keep track of them all. Do yourself a favour and try to work through things in their order of priority, or you'll get really irritated by the way they spiral out of control. It doesn't help that a certain person keeps trying to distract you from your own tasks with anxieties of their own.

● Wednesday 2 June ●

You're in a warm-hearted and generous mood today, especially when dealing with loved ones and members of the family. You want to give them as much of your time as possible, and also to do anything else that will keep them happy. The only snag will come if you're trying to spread yourself too thin and you end up making promises that will be difficult, if not impossible, to keep. You may forget all about them but other people won't.

• *Thursday 3 June* •

It's a red-letter day for your relationships because you're facing some important and far-reaching changes to some of them. If you've known for some time that things simply aren't working out in the way you want with you-know-who, you're about to reach a crisis point at which it becomes screamingly obvious that the present situation can't continue for much longer. You may have to be cruel to be kind, or much more forceful than you would like, in order to get your point across. But do you really have any viable alternative?

• *Friday 4 June* •

Do a little lateral thinking today and it will work wonders. Don't feel hidebound because you're supposed to do things in a certain way: you have a great opportunity to try a different approach for a change. Even so, you may have to play down your unorthodox technique when talking to anyone who sticks rigidly to convention.

• *Saturday 5 June* •

You're receptive to all sorts of ideas and influences today, so enjoy opening your mind to some of the many wonders that the world has to offer. You could be enthralled by a spiritual or religious topic or belief, or become engrossed in ways to make the world a better place. Don't underestimate what happens to you now: it will have a powerful effect on you if you let it.

• *Sunday 6 June* •

Today is a great day for talking about the ideas that occurred to you yesterday. But you should choose your audience carefully because you don't want to chat to anyone who will pour cold water on your ideas or make you feel like an idiot. You also don't want to get on your soapbox and feel that you've got to convert everyone you encounter, because that won't go down well.

• *Monday 7 June* •

This is another heady day in which you enjoy letting your mind wander in all sorts of exciting directions. You may decide that you can't live another moment without buying a book on your chosen new subject, or you might want to enrol in an evening class that will teach you more about it. The prospect of travel is also very appealing now, so how about it?

• *Tuesday 8 June* •

You're blessed with an astonishing amount of charm and tact today, making you quite a force to be reckoned with. In fact, if you're trying to sweet-talk someone into submission you should be carrying a government health warning because it will be almost impossible for anyone to resist you, and they might even find you seriously addictive. Sounds fun!

• *Wednesday 9 June* •

You want to branch out in new directions today and you won't like it if anyone tries to restrict you or make you toe the line in some way. Right now, you have a powerful need for carte blanche when making your own decisions and following your instincts. Some of your ideas may seem outrageous or highly controversial, yet you'll still want to pursue them, and that's exactly what you should do at the moment.

• *Thursday 10 June* •

You're thinking big today and it's really exciting. All sorts of possibilities are open to you and the last thing you want is to feel hampered. If you're currently facing huge obstacles or problems, you'll do your utmost to find a way round them. However, it's important that you keep at least one foot on the ground, or you could get embroiled in projects that are so unrealistic that they'll simply turn out to be a waste of time.

• *Friday 11 June* •

At least one of your relationships is currently at a very sensitive point and you're reminded of that very forcefully today. The tension between you and a certain person is so strong that it could almost feel like a life and death struggle, or something which will transform you for ever. Even if your heart is breaking, look on this period as a vital metamorphosis in your life.

• *Saturday 12 June* •

What a strange month this is turning out to be! You're feeling pulled in two directions: on the one hand you're grappling with powerful emotions about some of your relationships, and on the other your mind is expanding in some very exciting directions. This is a day for taking refuge in the bigger picture and in finding sense in what's happening to you right now.

• *Sunday 13 June* •

Discussions and conversations flow like silk today. You're eager to put across your ideas but you also want to hear what other people think. If possible, you should find some time to yourself and either put your thoughts down on paper or read an inspirational book that will help you to gain some insight into the experiences you're going through at the moment.

• Monday 14 June •

This is a good day for getting down to the nuts and bolts of your life. For instance, you might want to check your bank statement and make sure it's in order, or chase up some other financial arrangement in case it's hit a snag. If you're out shopping you'll want to hunt out some bargains and are definitely not in the mood to squander your hard-earned cash.

• Tuesday 15 June •

There are times when it's best to maintain a diplomatic silence and times when you need to speak up, and today you definitely need to say what you think. However, you must know what you're getting into, so don't provoke someone into a bout of verbal fisticuffs and then wonder what you've done to deserve such a tongue-lashing. You'll be getting as good as you give, so be careful.

• Wednesday 16 June •

Maybe it's simply reaction to the current events but today you want to thumb your nose at anyone who's being a stick-in-the-mud or a bore. Mind how you do this because the atmosphere at the moment is so tricky that you could stir up a lot more trouble than you anticipated. So kick against the traces in harmless ways that won't frighten the horses and land you in hot water.

• Thursday 17 June •

Today's New Moon marks the start of your personal new year, so treat it as an opportunity to embark on a fresh chapter in your life. The world is your oyster right now, even if it doesn't feel that way, so be brave and rise to the challenge of initiating new experiences and encounters that will lead on to better things. If you need to boost your self-confidence, consider giving yourself a makeover so that you'll know you're looking your best.

• *Friday 18 June* •

The best way to deal with everything you're currently going through is to talk about it. There is so much that you need to get off your chest that you probably won't know where to start. But do you know when to finish? Watch out for a possible tendency today to talk the hind legs off several donkeys, and change the conversation if you see someone's eyes starting to glaze over.

• *Saturday 19 June* •

Let's face it, Gemini, you need some light relief and it's just arrived. Today is a wonderful day for revelling in your home comforts or in anything else that makes you feel all warm and cosy inside. You might want to eat the entire contents of your fridge or cake tin, or go out for a calorie-laden meal; that may be the right move if it helps to soothe your fragile emotions.

• *Sunday 20 June* •

Someone is ready to fight like a tiger for what they believe in today, and you could be astonished by the vehemence of their reactions if they start to feel vulnerable. Of course, you may be the person who's so ready to spring to your own defence, in which case you should try not to over-react or set up a situation in which someone feels they have to retaliate.

• *Monday 21 June* •

During the coming four weeks you'll be concentrating on your values and priorities in life, especially if you need to restructure these or give them more importance than they've enjoyed in the past. This is not something to be taken lightly, especially if you need every ounce of comfort you can find right now. So focus on activities and people that make you feel good about yourself.

• *Tuesday 22 June* •

This is a great day for reminding everyone how clever and innovative you can be in the right circumstances. It will be exhilarating to show a new side to yourself and also to hatch some brilliant schemes. You're at your best when thinking about how to push ahead with your career and long-term plans, and also how to make your money go further.

• *Wednesday 23 June* •

The next few weeks are going to keep you very busy, and at times there will be never a dull moment. This will be just what the doctor ordered if you're currently wondering what to do with yourself or you're trying to fill a huge gap in your life. Local events and neighbourhood activities will occupy a prominent place in your diary.

• *Thursday 24 June* •

Someone is very persuasive and stubborn today, and they're determined to get their own way come what may. Your best bet is to let them get on with it all by themselves, and to leave them alone until they've come to their senses again. Try not to get drawn into a battle of wills because it will be emotionally exhausting and you won't get anywhere.

• *Friday 25 June* •

Do you want to swell the coffers in some way? Then put on your thinking cap today and you'll come up with some good ideas. If you're currently involved in a property deal or home improvement plan, this is a great day for taking another look at your budget and making sure it's still viable. However, you must resist the temptation to allocate yourself more money if you know you really can't afford it.

• Saturday 26 June •

One of your favourite people pays you a massive compliment today or does something else that makes you feel loved and appreciated. This may not be a world-shattering event but it will cheer you up nonetheless and bring a pretty blush to your cheek. A little retail therapy may be in order now, in which case you'll adore treating yourself to some new clothes or make-up.

• Sunday 27 June •

You need to face some financial facts today, even if they aren't very palatable. So if you know you've been overspending this month, you should do something about it now. But take care that you don't simply feel paralysed by panic and end up worrying about it rather than doing something constructive. You may also have to cope with someone who can't help criticizing you.

• Monday 28 June •

You're longing to show a new side to your character today, so what do you have in mind? If you're usually worried about playing a part, living up to your reputation, or setting a good example, you'll want to put all that to one side for the time being and just do what comes naturally. The more strait-laced you usually are, the more liberating this will feel. Maybe you should do it more often!

• *Tuesday 29 June* •

This is a super day for making a big effort to get on well with colleagues and other people you meet through the course of your work. So instead of feeling your heart sink when you have to talk to the resident bore, do your best to make them sparkle. You'll be astonished when you succeed, yet delighted to find that this person has hidden depths. You may not want to plumb them very often but it's good to know that they're there.

• *Wednesday 30 June* •

You're ready to put a lot of zest and energy into the day's activities, especially if they involve rushing around from one place to another. You'll enjoy being busily and productively occupied, and you'll be amazed at how much you manage to get done. In fact, whenever the pace slackens you'll start to feel slightly restless and bored, wondering what you can do next.

JULY AT A GLANCE

Love	♥ ♥ ♥
Money	£ $ £ $ £
Career	💻 💻
Health	☼ ☼

• *Thursday 1 July* •

Your relationship with a certain person gets rather tense today and you'll have to tread carefully. They're taking things a bit too seriously for your liking and you get the distinct impression that they could become quite worked up given half a chance. Do your best not to make the situation worse by unintentionally implying things that are guaranteed to get this other person in a right old lather.

• *Friday 2 July* •

Today's Full Moon signals that it's time for you to pay attention to your finances, particularly in the area of joint resources. For instance, if you've been meaning to work out who owes what with your partner, get it all out of the way during the coming fortnight. The next two weeks are also a good opportunity to clear the air with a close partner if problems are leading to recriminations or resentments.

• *Saturday 3 July* •

If you want to follow yesterday's advice and sort out your financial situation, this is a very good day for getting out all the relevant paperwork and checking that you've got all the facts at your disposal. If you need to formulate your argument or put forward your case you'll manage to do it now, but try not to get bogged down in petty details that will only cloud the issue or give the impression that you've got an axe to grind.

• *Sunday 4 July* •

You're at your most voluble and eloquent between now and the 25th, which means you'll be quite something. This will be a fabulous opportunity to put forward your ideas and share them with others, although you'll have to resist the tendency to hog the conversation and not let anyone even draw breath. It will also be a chance to get to know some of your neighbours better.

• *Monday 5 July* •

Today is a good day for spending money and effort on your home and family, especially if you're hoping to make things more comfortable for everyone. If you're currently in the throes of moving house, things will go surprisingly well right now and people will be a lot more helpful than they are usually. You might even have a stroke of financial luck.

• *Tuesday 6 July* •

You feel able to rely on a certain person today, safe in the knowledge that they'll do what they can to help you. They might give you some excellent advice, open some doors on your behalf, or introduce you to someone who'll be very influential. If you've been thinking about looking for a job that offers better pay or greater satisfaction, keep your eyes peeled for it right now.

• *Wednesday 7 July* •

Hmm! A certain someone has the bit between their teeth today and they won't let go. They're getting very heated about something and, to hear them talk, you'd think it was the most important thing on the face of this earth. You disagree, of course, which is where the trouble will start. Let them get all worked up if necessary, but don't join in or encourage them.

• *Thursday 8 July* •

Pay attention to your money matters today and you'll achieve a great deal. That might mean paying bills or devising a budget to carry you through the rest of the month, but whatever you do now will be time well spent. You'll prefer to err on the side of caution rather than take risks, and it certainly makes sense to be prudent at the moment.

• *Friday 9 July* •

If you're going out on the town today, make sure that every-one has a rough idea of how much it's going to cost. Otherwise there could be some difficult scenes when someone cuts up rough about paying their share. This isn't the day for anyone to brag or boast about their financial position or any of their possessions, as that will lead to ill feeling from everyone else.

• Saturday 10 July •

Is there something you want to say? Then you'll have no problems in getting it off your chest today, especially if it calls for courage or initiative. Actually, the difficulty will be in knowing when to shut up because you'll have a tendency to say too much or hammer your point home. It will be tempting to be sarcastic or cutting, but what good will that do?

• Sunday 11 July •

Do you have a nasty suspicion that you went over the top yesterday? Then make amends now, while you're feeling so articulate and diplomatic. If you can't talk your way out of trouble then start apologizing profusely – but make sure you mean it. You'll enjoy getting some fresh air at some point, especially if you can go for a walk in some beautiful surroundings.

• Monday 12 July •

Honesty is your best policy today, and if you try to cover something up you'll only come unstuck sooner or later. Sitting on the fence could also lead to misunderstandings, so it would be better to say what you think than try to fudge the issue. If you're involved in a charity or good cause, this isn't a good day to launch a new project: it will encounter endless hassles.

• Tuesday 13 July •

A certain someone may sound plausible, but believe them at your peril. They may simply have got their facts wrong, even though they think they're telling you the truth, but there's a strong chance that they're perfectly well aware that they're spinning you a line. If you're out and about, keep a beady eye on your belongings in case something gets mislaid or is pinched.

• *Wednesday 14 July* •

The current emphasis is on your communications and you really excel at them today. You know exactly what to say and when to say it, so make the most of this silver-tongued phase while it lasts. Take full advantage of it by writing letters, sending e-mails, or getting involved in negotiations or discussions. Alternatively, simply enjoy nattering to whoever is around.

• *Thursday 15 July* •

If you've been waiting to hear about a pay rise or bonus, there could be some surprise news on its way to you. In fact, surprises are the order of the day because there's no knowing what's going to happen next. Don't worry – you're unlikely to encounter anything tricky or problematic. Instead, you'll need to be flexible and able to switch from one activity to the next at a moment's notice.

• *Friday 16 July* •

Keep well clear of anyone who makes a habit of subtly putting you down or pointing out your faults because they'll be even more adept at it than usual today. But you must also do your best to be aware of the messages you're sending out because you may have a tendency to make people feel guilty about something or to play the martyr, even if you don't realize you're doing it.

• *Saturday 17 July* •

Some of your relationships haven't exactly been plain sailing lately, but today you at least get the chance to talk about what's happening. In fact, some of your conversations could be highly productive and searching, so you're left in no doubt about where you stand. If you're currently trying to get to the bottom of a mystery, you should be able to crack it now.

• *Sunday 18 July* •

This is a day for enjoying your local surroundings whenever possible. That might mean strolling around your nearest park or beach, visiting the shops or seeing what's going on in your neighbourhood. If you're able to choose the company you keep today, opt for people who you know like the back of your hand because you won't want to make a huge effort with anyone.

• *Monday 19 July* •

No sooner does an idea pop into your head today than it lands on the tip of your tongue, and you find you've put it into words. Now, this might be marvellous, especially if your intuition is helping you to find exactly the right words at the right time. But if you start to get irritable or flustered you may find that you're dropping clangers or being far too blunt. So calm down!

• *Tuesday 20 July* •

You've been enjoying carrying out some home improvements recently and this is another day for splashing out and letting rip. Watch out if you're going near the shops because it will be incredibly tempting to forget about your budget and splurge on anything you fancy. You'll be drawn to luxurious objects, and unfortunately they probably come with a hefty price tag.

• *Thursday 29 July* •

Turn your attention to your finances today, especially if you want to check that a project hasn't gone over budget or you're currently devising a new fiscal strategy. If you're waiting for a payment, today is a good opportunity to chase it up, but you'll make more progress if you're polite and considerate than if you're heavy-handed or threatening.

• *Friday 30 July* •

It's difficult to keep things in perspective today because they have such a strong tendency to overwhelm or depress you. This is especially true when it comes to your finances, because right now they seem almost too ghastly to contemplate. Whether the situation is really as dire as it appears is neither here nor there as far as you're concerned because you simply can't help taking the bleakest possible view. Even so, try not to lose sleep over it.

• *Saturday 31 July* •

Today's Full Moon acts as a reminder that certain situations aren't nearly as cut and dried as you might like to think. So do your best not to fall into the trap of thinking that a delicate problem is easy to solve and getting angry when people fail to tackle it in the way you suggest. You may even have to eat your words at some point, which will give you mental indigestion.

AUGUST AT A GLANCE

Love	♥ ♥
Money	£ $
Career	💻 💻
Health	☼ ☼

• Sunday 1 August •

How wacky and unpredictable are you prepared to be today? It looks as though you're happy to go out on a limb if that will get your point across, but there's a problem in this because it means you're likely to get right up someone's nose. You could easily say things that are deliberately intended to cause a stir or shock someone, but this will backfire on you sooner or later. Yes, you want to rebel, but you must be careful how you do it.

• Monday 2 August •

Be very careful when dealing with people in authority today because the atmosphere will be fraught and irritable. If you're trying to toe the line with them you'll be annoyed about it, and may unconsciously say the wrong thing. You'll also get very bogged down in details if you're sorting out paperwork or filling in forms, so do your best to remain objective. If the worst comes to the worst, have a break from what you're doing so you can clear your head.

• Tuesday 3 August •

If you're feeling guilty about what's been happening over the past couple of days, you'll now want to make amends and may even go over the top in the process. If some grovelling is required then that's what you need to do, but try not to get into someone's good books again by promising them the earth because you'll only have to let them down when you fail to deliver the goods.

• *Wednesday 4 August* •

Is someone indulging in some attention-seeking behaviour today? You must admit that it looks that way to you, because they're doing things designed to make all eyes swivel in their direction. Unfortunately, they'll make more and more of a fuss until they get what they want. They may even have an emotional outburst at the most inconvenient time.

• *Thursday 5 August* •

It's been a difficult month so far but things look much more easy-going today, thank goodness. This is a marvellous day for taking part in social activities and mixing with as many people as possible. You're feeling gregarious and outgoing, and will enjoy catching up with people you haven't seen lately. It's an especially good day for getting together with friends and neighbours.

• *Friday 6 August* •

During the last couple of months it's been made perfectly clear to you that certain relationships need very careful evaluation, and that it's only a matter of time before some vital changes are made. Well, this is a day for a major transformation in a relationship, provided it will be to everyone's benefit. Resist the temptation to do things in which only you will benefit.

• *Saturday 7 August* •

Beware of an extravagant streak that takes control of you from today and lasts until early September. It will encourage you to spend money like water, and also to splash out on all sorts of treats and luxuries. You won't want to stint yourself, and that will cause problems if you're supposed to be carefully controlling your budget.

• *Sunday 8 August* •

Spend time with loved ones today if possible. Being with your nearest and dearest is exactly what you're in the mood for, especially if you can take care of them or spoil them in some way. If you're cooking, you'll have a tendency to make much more food than anyone can eat; resist the temptation to scoff all the leftovers when no one's looking.

• *Monday 9 August* •

Someone is being awfully defensive and edgy today, making it difficult to talk to them without feeling that you're being put on the spot or they're waiting for you to say the wrong thing. This is especially likely when talking to members of the family. Bear this in mind if you'll be spending time with a relative who always seems to be hovering on the brink of a major huff.

• *Tuesday 10 August* •

Domestic relationships start to come under strain from today and they won't sort themselves out until the beginning of September. Be very wary of misreading situations and try not to give anyone the wrong impression simply because you haven't said something important. Do your best to avoid signing any documents or agreements until this tricky phase blows over, in case you're being led up the garden path or you haven't been given all the facts.

• *Wednesday 11 August* •

It's a super day for going shopping because you've got plenty of energy for tearing around the shops and seeing what's on offer. You're also interested in getting to grips with some energetic domestic chores, such as gardening or housework. You'll really put your back into them all, and you'll be thrilled with the great results.

• *Thursday 12 August* •

Today is the perfect day for taking part in some form of negotiation or discussion because you're perfectly prepared to put your thoughts into words in whichever way will be most helpful and straightforward. Right now, you have no desire to hedge your bets or pull the wool over anyone's eyes, and you'll be very annoyed if they do this sort of thing to you.

• *Friday 13 August* •

There's no need to be superstitious about today's date because things will go really well. In fact, there could be some lovely surprises in store, especially if you've currently got your sights set on someone older, richer or more influential than you. You might also hear some unexpected good news about a financial matter that is working out to your advantage.

• *Saturday 14 August* •

Right now you've got a hankering for anything and anyone that's cosy, familiar and unchallenging. You need all the emotional security you can get today, so you'll naturally gravitate towards people who you know inside out and will be slightly wary of meeting anyone for the first time. You might also want to do some serious comfort eating at some point.

• *Sunday 15 August* •

Concentrate on your priorities in life today, because they'll make you feel good. They will also remind you that there is more to life than hard grind and problems. After all, you've had a very difficult couple of months and you're overdue for some light relief. So pamper yourself in some way and your cares will vanish for the time being.

• Monday 16 August •

Today's New Moon is putting the accent on your communications, so think about how you can improve these during the rest of the month. You might decide that it's time you got yourself a new phone, for instance, or it could be your cue to improve your current computer in some way. This will also be an ace opportunity to call a truce with someone if you've been at daggers drawn.

• Tuesday 17 August •

You're blessed with a very practical approach to life today, particularly when it comes to anything connected with your home or finances. And if you can combine the two in some way then you'll really strike it lucky. If you're currently involved in a property deal, things will go in your favour and you might even end up much better off.

• Wednesday 18 August •

Someone dear to your heart has a habit of shooting from the hip and saying whatever pops into their head today. As a result you could hear some rather uncomfortable home truths, and this person won't seem to care what effect their words have on you. Don't they have any consideration for a person's feelings? Not at the moment, it seems. But maybe it's something you should listen to, all the same.

• *Thursday 19 August* •

Steady! A certain person has the uncanny ability of being able to wind you up like a spring today and they may not even need to use words, since their body language or general behaviour will be just as controversial. Before you completely lose your cool, ask yourself why they're determined to get you to rise to the bait and then don't give them the satisfaction of watching it happen.

• *Friday 20 August* •

If you ask someone's advice, be prepared for them to sound positively gloomy. They're taking the worst possible view of everything and will quickly infect you with their miserable view of the world. This isn't a good day to spend money because you'll suffer awful pangs of guilt afterwards, even if you know full well that you can afford to have a splurge.

• *Saturday 21 August* •

It's a day for making the most of your social life, and you won't have to stray far afield in order to do so. You'll enjoy taking part in a local event or neighbourhood activity, and will do your best to make the whole thing go with a swing. If you haven't spoken to one of your favourite people lately, pick up the phone, or send them an e-mail to let them know you're thinking of them.

• *Sunday 22 August* •

During the next four weeks you'll want to devote plenty of time to your home and family. You may also be surprisingly reluctant to stray too far from your own front door, but that's exactly as it should be right now because you're in the mood for familiar faces and places. Anything or anyone that offers comfort and emotional security will be all right by you.

• *Monday 23 August* •

Gather some of your loved ones around you and talk to them. You're in the mood for some clever conversation, although that might be rather difficult if certain people get their own way and manage to hog the limelight. You might also have more visitors or phone calls than usual, so get set for a day full of pleasant interruptions and little incidents.

• *Tuesday 24 August* •

The emotional temperature is climbing up the scale today, leading to a rather intense hothouse atmosphere. A partner might get a bee in their bonnet about something, making them determined to bang on about it for as long as possible and probably make you feel wretched about it at the same time. Try to handle the situation with graciousness and understanding.

• *Wednesday 25 August* •

Mind your Ps and Qs over the next few days because there's a strong chance that you'll accidentally say the wrong thing or send out the wrong signals. Misunderstandings will be rife, and there could also be other communication glitches such as letters that get mislaid, phone calls that aren't answered and gadgets that go on the blink. If you've got to write an important letter, it might be wise to delay it until 2 September, when things get back to normal.

• *Thursday 26 August* •

This is a great day for talking about your feelings and allowing loved ones to do the same in return. Look on it as the chance to get things out into the open, particularly if they've had a tendency to be swept under the carpet or to provoke arguments.

The more honest and open you can be now, the better for everyone concerned.

• *Friday 27 August* •

You are absolutely determined to remind a certain person that you're an individual in your own right and that you want the freedom to be able to do your own thing. You'll cut up rough if you think you're being restricted in some way, especially by someone else's expectations or worldly responsibilities that have been put on your shoulders. You're longing to rebel, but be careful how you do this. You don't want to give yourself a bad name.

• *Saturday 28 August* •

It will be difficult to concentrate today because your mind is on other things. In fact, you're floating off into a world of your own at every opportunity, and this will mean you come across as very absent-minded and vague. You're keen to tune in to the atmosphere around you, and you'll be very good at this. So trust your instincts and listen to what they're telling you.

• *Sunday 29 August* •

Someone seems to be a walking encyclopedia, judging by their determination to hurl facts and figures at you. You'll very soon lose interest but will they stop talking? No, they won't. Try to resist the temptation to engage them in a battle of words in which the winner is the one who talks longest and loudest. Maybe you could change the subject to something more interesting?

• *Monday 30 August* •

You've been feeling very agitated about certain responsibilities and expectations lately, and today's Full Moon is encouraging you to reach some sober decisions about them. If you feel they're running your life and making it a misery then maybe it's time to reduce the number of obligations that have fallen on your shoulders.

• Tuesday 31 August •

Emotionally, you're in a very vulnerable position today because you're highly sensitive to any hint of rejection from other people. You may even imagine that you're being given the cold shoulder when this isn't what's happening at all. If you've got the money, it's a great day for investing it sensibly in schemes that will grow in value over the years.

SEPTEMBER AT A GLANCE

Love	♥ ♥ ♥ ♥ ♥
Money	£ $ £
Career	💻 💻
Health	☼ ☼

• Wednesday 1 September •

You're feeling very sympathetic towards the plight of others today and will do your best to help anyone who's going through a bad time. You may even know that someone is in trouble without them having to tell you because somehow you'll pick it up through their mood or body language. But you must remember that while you can sympathize, you may not be able to wave a magic wand and make everything better.

• *Thursday 2 September* •

Communications haven't been easy recently so it will come as a great relief to you to know that they begin to get back on track from today. In fact, this is a marvellous opportunity to be decisive and put forward your ideas, provided that you know what you're doing. At some point today you'll enjoy relaxing with some of your nearest and dearest, and you could be tempted to push the boat out in some way.

• *Friday 3 September* •

It's a day for enjoying your home comforts and not doing anything too strenuous. You might fancy doing a bit of gardening or tidying up around the house but you'll draw the line at slogging your guts out. If you know that a loved one needs a shoulder to cry on this is a very good day for drawing them to one side and encouraging them to confide in you.

• *Saturday 4 September* •

Take care, because you're easily distracted today and could easily get into a bit of a muddle. Your mind is on other things and you also want to shy away from anything that seems to be too much trouble or very demanding. There could be a mix-up with an older friend or relative who isn't being clear about what they expect from you. Have you thought of asking them outright?

• *Sunday 5 September* •

Once again, it's difficult to handle older people with much grace because such strange things are going on between you. But today, you'll have to cope with someone who is being a law unto themselves or is behaving very erratically. Even though this will be unsettling and irritating, there may not be much you can do about it, other than to grin and bear it. Is that really so hard?

• *Monday 6 September* •

The atmosphere between you and a certain person is so thick that you can almost see it. What's wrong? Perhaps a past resentment has reared its ugly head once again, or one of you is seething about something that's only just happened. Unfortunately, it's the sort of day in which you're both more likely to sulk and brood than to say what's bugging you.

• *Tuesday 7 September* •

You're feeling bright and bubbly today, and yesterday's dark mood has entirely evaporated. Today is a wonderful chance to make contact with as many people as possible because you're in such a charming and lively frame of mind. If you need to say something tactfully, do it now and you won't have any problems at all.

• *Wednesday 8 September* •

If a duty or obligation has been getting you down recently, this is a good day to think about how you might lighten the load or alter your attitude towards it. Try to approach the whole thing from a fresh angle and see if that makes a difference. There could also be a nice surprise when someone shows their appreciation of all your recent efforts and hard work.

• *Thursday 9 September* •

You're in nest-building mode today, and will really enjoy making your home look and feel more cosy. If you're going past the shops you could be drawn to items that will increase the comfort of your home or add to its appearance. It's also a nice day for simply pottering around your local supermarket and seeing what's on offer, then cooking a delicious meal for your nearest and dearest.

• *Friday 10 September* •

Watch out! A certain person is in a very wilful and self-centred state today, and they'll walk all over you given half a chance. It will be difficult to know how to handle this for the best. If you stand up to them you could have quite a fight on your hands, but if you let them get their own way you'll be setting a damaging precedent. Either way, don't provoke their anger unless it's inevitable, as you might unleash something very powerful.

• *Saturday 11 September* •

Oh dear! You strongly suspect that someone thinks they're on the road to sainthood today and they want everyone else to know it. For instance, they might do someone a favour and then tell everyone all about it. Do your best to avoid falling into the same trap of doing something for others and then convincing yourself that it shows what a wonderful person you are.

• *Sunday 12 September* •

Profound and far-reaching changes are dogging your footsteps at the moment and this is another day when you come up against the need to make some sweeping alterations to your life. You won't find this easy and you'll also have to cope with opposition from certain quarters but you know what you must do, and right now you have to steel yourself to get on with it.

• Monday 13 September •

Someone who normally commands your respect has been behaving very strangely since the start of August, leaving you in the unenviable position of trying to guess what they're going to do next. Well, they're up to their old tricks again today but this time you stand a better chance of discovering what's going on. But it may be very different from what you've imagined.

• Tuesday 14 September •

Family matters haven't exactly been a barrel of laughs lately but today's New Moon is offering you the chance to set the record straight, put the past behind you and do your best to spread the spirit of peace and forgiveness. Yes, this may well be a poignant and heart-searching time, but do you really want to cope with this atmosphere of seething resentment any longer?

• Wednesday 15 September •

You have a lot of energy at your disposal today, and the burning question is how you're going to use it. Try your hardest to turn it to productive and constructive ends, such as having a blitz on the housework or garden. This will help you to avoid getting irritable and argumentative, which is more than likely to happen if you spend the day in sedentary or boring pursuits.

• Thursday 16 September •

A heart-to-heart with a loved one works out really well today, provided you're both prepared to say what you think while still considering the other one's feelings. If you're involved in the early stages of a romantic relationship, this will be a delightful day in which you edge closer together, whether physically, emotionally or both.

• *Friday 17 September* •

You're blessed with a lot of common sense today, so turn it to your advantage. It's an excellent opportunity to do some financial planning or to lay down the foundations of a money-making scheme that will grow in time. Right now you aren't interested in anything that's risky or dodgy and it wouldn't go well even if you tried it, but you'll succeed with solid, sensible schemes.

• *Saturday 18 September* •

A certain person is being very idealistic today, because they've set their sights on something or someone that is virtually unattainable. If you try to tell them this they won't listen or they'll accuse you of being a spoilsport, so you may have to reconcile yourself to watching them break their heart and then helping them to pick up the pieces.

• *Sunday 19 September* •

Have a look around your home today and see if you can think of any ways to improve it. Maybe all it needs is a good clean, or perhaps you'll realize that it's about time you got out the paint pots and gave it a facelift. If you work from home, this is a good opportunity to improve your surroundings in some way, even if that simply means making them more neat and tidy.

• *Monday 20 September* •

Guess who isn't exactly the most pleasant companion today. They're in a bad mood and they're coming out with some cutting comments that immediately put you on the defensive. Before you lay all the blame for this at their feet, consider how you may be contributing to the situation. Perhaps you're being sulky, provocative or equally sarcastic?

• *Tuesday 21 September* •

If you're currently making some domestic plans, you'll get so carried away today that it will be a struggle to keep your feet on the ground. Instead, you'll indulge in all sorts of wonderful flights of fancy, and may also dismiss current difficulties with an airy wave of your hand. You can be very imaginative today, Gemini, but don't lose all sense of reality in the process!

• *Wednesday 22 September* •

A certain person is eaten up with curiosity that could quickly turn to suspicion, making them grill you with all sorts of searching questions. It's as though they've already convinced themselves that you're guilty of something and they're now looking for the proof. This is bound to put you on the defensive but it would be better for you to ask them what they're playing at.

• *Thursday 23 September* •

The atmosphere has improved dramatically, thank goodness, and today you're in a very sunny and triumphant mood. You're keen to make the best of any situation in which you find yourself, and everyone around you will enjoy your optimism and bright outlook. It's a day for having fun, especially if that means venturing fairly far afield or visiting somewhere for the first time.

• *Friday 24 September* •

If you make a real effort to understand someone and get to know them better now, your relationship will take a giant step forward. This will be true whether you're neighbours, members of the same family, lovers or friends, and you'll benefit in many different ways as a result. But you must be prepared to be honest and open about your thoughts and feelings. No hedging your bets!

• *Saturday 25 September* •

Congratulations! From today you enter a delicious, year-long phase in which love will play a bigger part in your life and you'll have plenty of opportunities in which to shine. This will be no time to hide your creative gifts or indulge in false modesty, because this is when you can reveal fresh talents and abilities with a strong sense of pride and enjoyment.

• *Sunday 26 September* •

You've got your head screwed on the right way this Sunday, making it the perfect day for thinking about practical and financial matters. Right now you'd rather take a sober and careful approach to such things than do anything foolish, and that will turn out to be a very sensible strategy. It may not be terribly exciting but it will bring the sort of results you're looking for.

• *Monday 27 September* •

You're a real live wire today, with abundant energy and joie de vivre. There may even be times when you'll find it hard to sit still, and you'll certainly be happiest if you can keep on the go as much as possible. You're feeling competitive, making you want to thrash your opponent if you're taking part in a sporty or athletic activity. But don't go overboard and injure yourself.

• *Tuesday 28 September* •

Today's Full Moon is highlighting your friendships and also your hopes and dreams, helping you to identify any problems that need solving. For instance, you might realize that your relationship with a chum is languishing for lack of attention, making you want to make amends by spending more time with them. Or you may decide that a cherished plan needs a careful rethink.

• *Wednesday 29 September* •

Busy, busy, busy! You're rushing around so much today, and at such speed, that you'll probably meet yourself coming through a doorway. Right now you need to be as active as possible, both mentally and physically. In fact, you're at your most Geminian today because you need to have your fingers in lots of pies and you'll relish the chance to show how versatile and inventive you can be.

• *Thursday 30 September* •

Be warned that if you ask someone's advice about money today you'll get a disappointing reply. That might be because this person is talking sense and you need to listen to them. But unfortunately it's just as likely to be because they've developed a severe case of sour grapes that makes them want to pour cold water on your ideas and bring you down to their miserable level. Neither situation will be easy to deal with.

OCTOBER AT A GLANCE

Love	♥ ♥ ♥ ♥ ♥
Money	£ $
Career	💻 💻 💻 💻 💻
Health	☼ ☼ ☼ ☼ ☼

• Friday 1 October •

You know, someone is definitely kidding themselves at the moment about being holier than thou. You get another dose of it today and, despite its amusement value, it's starting to wear thin. Who does this person think they are? Do be careful that you don't get sucked into a competition with them to prove that you're just as wonderful. You don't have to sink to their level, do you?

• Saturday 2 October •

It's party time! Enjoyment is uppermost in your mind today and you'll find any excuse to let your hair down, open a couple of bottles and whoop it up. Ideally, you should do this with some of your favourite people because they'll help the whole thing to go with a swing, but you'll make a big effort to socialize with whoever happens to be around, whether they're loved ones or perfect strangers.

• Sunday 3 October •

Between now and the end of the month you'll gain a lot of emotional satisfaction from being with close family and friends. You'll love knowing that there's a strong bond between you, whether you're linked by blood or friendship. It's also going to be a great time to lavish some care and attention on your home.

• *Monday 4 October* •

Someone gets steamed up awfully easily today, making it rather draining to be around them for long because they're exuding so much intensity. They're taking everything very seriously and will read all sorts of meanings into the smallest incident. You may also behave this way now but do your best to keep a sense of perspective about the day's events and not to brood over them.

• *Tuesday 5 October* •

You've got a very open mind today, making you receptive to all sorts of ideas and concepts. You'll also enjoy exploring topics with a spiritual or mystical theme. However, you need to keep your feet on the ground and not be persuaded into believing things that are obviously a load of bunkum, because if that happens you could be duped in some way.

• *Wednesday 6 October* •

This isn't a good day for trusting to luck or crossing your fingers and hoping for the best, especially when dealing with anything connected with property, family matters and red tape. If you do that, you'll have to watch things spiral out of control. Instead, you must be adaptable and ready to think on your feet, and also to accept that someone may try to move the goalposts.

• *Thursday 7 October* •

This is the perfect day to tackle your finances but you need to keep your sense of humour while you're doing it, otherwise you'll end up feeling gloomy or worried. Yes, it's one of those days when anxieties seem to crawl out of the woodwork and grab you, leaving you fretting about all sorts of things that may never happen. So do your best to remain positive.

• *Friday 8 October* •

Your social life is keeping you busy at the moment and you're in great demand right now. It's a super day for keeping in touch with lots of different people, especially if that means cramming lots of short trips into your day. You've got bags of energy today and will enjoy having lunch with one person, tea with another and dinner with someone else. It's a day for being a true Gemini!

• *Saturday 9 October* •

There's a lot to talk about with a certain person today, and you've both got the chance to get down to the nitty-gritty of what's going on. If you can't do this face to face, get on the phone or send them a letter or e-mail, because it would be a shame to pass up a communications opportunity like this. Besides, you need to get various things off your chest, and the sooner the better.

• *Sunday 10 October* •

If you're doing some entertaining you'll have a wonderful time, and so will everyone else. Surround yourself with loved ones and revel in their company. The drink will flow, the food will be delicious, and everyone will look forward to another invitation from you very soon. So be careful – you may end up making a rod for your own back!

• *Monday 11 October* •

It was all sweetness and light with your nearest and dearest yesterday, but today it feels like negotiations to avoid hostilities breaking out. Perhaps someone is being possessive or controlling of you, and you don't like it, or maybe it's the other way round. Past resentments might also come between you, making you wonder if you'll ever be able to put them behind you.

• *Tuesday 12 October* •

Budgets and other financial strategies go very well today because you're in a money-minded mood. You're able to combine practicality with the ability to spend money when necessary, but you certainly won't be flinging it around in all directions and spending it on fripperies. If you're currently negotiating over property you'll make some clever moves now.

• *Wednesday 13 October* •

Everything was going really well yesterday but suddenly you're beset by doubts and worries over your finances. Perhaps someone has had a quiet word in your ear and set you thinking, or maybe you've had a nasty letter from your bank manager. On the other hand, maybe you're simply worrying about things that may never happen and getting yourself into a state over nothing?

• *Thursday 14 October* •

Today's eclipsed New Moon is just what you need because it signals great news for your love life. If you're currently single you might fall hook, line and sinker for Mr or Ms Wonderful any minute now. You might also hear some good news about a child or receive an invitation to a celebration over the next couple of weeks. This is also a great time to launch a new creative enterprise.

• *Friday 15 October* •

Put on your thinking cap about your work and health, and consider ways in which you can improve your current prospects. If you're a typical Gemini you have a tendency to take your health for granted, in which case the coming couple of weeks are a marvellous opportunity to find ways of boosting your general well-being. Maybe you should talk to a medical expert?

• *Saturday 16 October* •

You're feeling industrious and level-headed, and you'll really shine in any situation in which you have to be rational and practical. It's great if you're working today because you'll give a very good impression of cool, calm efficiency without becoming a robot. You may also want to tuck a colleague under your protective wing.

• *Sunday 17 October* •

Your Gemini brain is shining like gold today and working much faster than usual. It's therefore a wonderful opportunity to come up with new schemes and to hatch some inventive plans. You're in a very far-seeing state of mind, and you're also able to find your way round problems that might defeat you at other times. Good for you!

• *Monday 18 October* •

You're in a sunny mood, especially if you can be with some of your favourite people. Make the most of this happy influence while it lasts because the focus will soon switch to more work and less play. If you're hoping to make a big impression on a certain person, you'll be able to do it today without going overboard and putting them off.

• *Tuesday 19 October* •

Watch out if you're going shopping with someone else today because you'll persuade each other to spend much more money than you can comfortably part with. You'll spot all sorts of tempting treats and indulgences, and tell yourself that you simply can't live without them. Be especially careful not to overload your credit card with debts that you can't pay off.

• *Wednesday 20 October* •

Someone dear to your heart is feeling threatened today, and they'll react by being manipulative and tricky. It would be very easy to get drawn into the drama that they're trying to create, but do your best not to let this happen and concentrate instead on the emotions that lie behind this smokescreen that they've created. What's really going on with them?

• *Thursday 21 October* •

You're very interested in spiritual and mystical matters today, particularly if they bring you comfort or remind you that there's much more to life than run-of-the-mill concerns. How about giving yourself a tarot reading, consulting an astrological web site, or visiting somewhere that feels special or sacred?

• *Friday 22 October* •

Today's positive and upbeat mood will rub off on everyone who comes within sniffing distance of you, so don't be surprised if they're reluctant to leave your side. Use your current energy to get ahead with challenging or difficult projects that normally sap your strength. Right now, you've got the stamina and impetus to tackle them and make a success of them.

• *Saturday 23 October* •

Whatever you're doing today, you'll have to work hard to concentrate because your thoughts are floating off in all directions. So, if you're washing up you should concentrate on that and nothing else. If you're at work, focus your mind on that and screen out all distracting trains of thought. You must also try not to let certain people put you off your stroke, whether deliberately or accidentally.

• *Sunday 24 October* •

Yikes! Someone has a real urge for power and they want to bend you to their will. They won't be very pleased if you refuse to play ball, but do you really want to feel that you're the puppet and they're pulling the strings? Of course not! It may be politic to make yourself scarce until they've calmed down again and are no longer being so controlling.

• *Monday 25 October* •

It will be very easy to find that you're piggy in the middle between the twin demands of work and home today. Both areas of life will have a strong claim on your time and attention, and there could be some emotional drains on your energy as well. The best way to handle this is to find a balance and sense of moderation, and not to make it an all-or-nothing situation.

• *Tuesday 26 October* •

This is a super day for spending money wisely and well on your home and family. You're in a canny mood, making you happy to invest your cash on items that represent good value for money but reluctant to squander it on fripperies or passing fancies. You'll also get the chance to remind someone how important they are to you, especially if they're down in the dumps.

• *Wednesday 27 October* •

You're much more powerful and impressive than you give yourself credit for today, so use this energy with care and consideration. Your words will have a strong effect on others, especially people who you're emotionally involved with, so try not to say things that you don't mean or which you know will upset them. Don't exploit your current power and influence.

• *Thursday 28 October* •

Worries and fears have been dogging your footsteps recently but today's eclipsed Full Moon gives you the chance to do something about them. Instead of lying awake at night fretting, or even being too scared to acknowledge the difficulties you're facing, you have no choice but to take a long, hard look at whatever is bugging you and then take some constructive action.

• *Friday 29 October* •

You'll be astonished by the amount of charm you have at your disposal between now and late November, and it's certainly going to turn a few heads. In fact, you might even collect a string of admirers as a result. If you're already involved with someone, use the next few weeks to add some fresh sparkle to your relationship and to really enjoy the love you share.

• *Saturday 30 October* •

Are you feeling lucky? Although it isn't advisable to bet your shirt or risk anything you can't afford to lose, it looks as though you could strike lucky today. So why not buy yourself a lottery or raffle ticket, or try your hand at a competition or quiz? You could also be lucky in love now, provided you don't raise the stakes too high.

• *Sunday 31 October* •

Fancy a rest? It's the sort of day when you'll be happiest if you can put your feet up and let the rest of the world carry on without you. If you do decide to venture outside your front door you'll enjoy visiting somewhere with a mysterious or mystical atmosphere, or talking to someone who has a very special view of the world.

NOVEMBER AT A GLANCE

Love	♥ ♥
Money	£ $ £ $ £
Career	💻 💻 💻 💻 💻
Health	☀ ☀ ☀ ☀ ☀

• *Monday 1 November* •

Believe it or not, 2005 is only around the corner and this is a great day for thinking about what you want to achieve in the year ahead. Don't be afraid to aim further than usual or to consider options that would normally seem far-fetched or too ambitious. Right now, you have fabulous clarity of vision and know exactly what you're capable of, given half a chance.

• *Tuesday 2 November* •

If you've been considering applying for a loan, changing bank accounts or making any other financial moves but haven't yet done anything about them, get cracking today. You'll manage to sort things out very easily, whether that means doing some research, asking questions or filling in forms. What's more, everyone you speak to will be surprisingly helpful.

• *Wednesday 3 November* •

Continue where you left off yesterday because once again you're in the mood to make things happen financially. You're still in a very sensible frame of mind so there's little danger of you taking on a bigger financial commitment than you can handle. Even so, you want to make sure you're putting your money to good use and you may decide to seek someone's advice, just to make sure.

• *Thursday 4 November* •

If you're a typical Gemini you're very skilled at communicating with others and your abilities will really come into their own throughout the rest of November. If there have been problems with a certain person lately your best chance of solving them is to talk about them and discuss them in detail. But make sure you listen to what partners are telling you.

• *Friday 5 November* •

Whoopee! You're in the mood for a celebration and you'll be the life and soul of the party. Play your cards right and this will turn out to be one of the nicest days of the entire month. As for your love life, if you're lucky you'll score ten out of ten with you-know-who. So make the most of your current high spirits and live every moment to the full. You deserve it!

• *Saturday 6 November* •

Is someone being brilliant or barmy? It's difficult to tell because they're completely off the wall right now and you can't make head or tail of what they're saying. There's also a chance that they're deliberately trying to wind you up by saying things that will make your hackles rise. If you start to behave this way, be prepared for the consequences.

• *Sunday 7 November* •

You need all the patience you can muster today, especially if you're trying to make progress at work or in a money matter. You'll encounter all sorts of obstacles or delays, and these will be so irritating that you'll want to tear your hair out. Don't waste your energy raging against things or people you can't control, or you'll end up feeling totally exhausted.

• *Monday 8 November* •

Life has so much to offer today that you feel quite moved by everything that's available to you. This might even have such a profound effect on you that you want to share your good fortune with people who aren't as lucky as you. It also promises to be a marvellous day emotionally, and a certain person might make one of your dreams come true. Definitely a day to write home about!

• *Tuesday 9 November* •

This is a super day for putting across your point of view and listening to other people's responses. In fact, you could have some interesting conversations, in which you bounce ideas off each other. Any form of negotiation or discussion will therefore go well now, and might lead to some very positive opportunities that might otherwise have passed you by. So keep talking and listening!

• *Wednesday 10 November* •

Some of your relationships haven't exactly been plain sailing lately but this is a day for pouring a little oil on troubled waters. Although this is unlikely to make all the problems magically go away, at least it will make you feel more positive about what's happening and will also enable you to get a better idea of what is going on with the other people who are involved.

• Thursday 11 November •

You're feeling very positive at the moment and today is no exception. You'll enjoy sharing your bright ideas and optimistic thoughts with whoever happens to be around. You may even manage to persuade a certain someone to change their mind and adopt a more upbeat attitude, but don't use this as an excuse for browbeating them into submission.

• Friday 12 November •

The coming fortnight gives you a fabulous opportunity to make some changes to your general state of health, so think about what would benefit you the most. Should you improve your diet so that you eat more sensibly or regularly? Could you incorporate more exercise into your daily schedule? Do you need to stop burning the candle at both ends? Or maybe all of the above apply?

• Saturday 13 November •

Make the most of your intuition and instincts today because they'll be spot on. You'll pick up all sorts of impressions from the atmosphere around you. However, you should keep your feet on the ground and not allow your imagination to take over and point you in misleading directions. You must also distinguish between reality and wishful thinking.

• *Sunday 14 November* •

What a chatterbox you are today! Your idea of heaven right now is to yak away to whoever happens to be around, and you won't mind if you're talking about deep and meaningful topics or simply discussing the weather. If there has been a nasty breach between you and a certain someone recently, this would be the perfect day to extend an olive branch and call a truce.

• *Monday 15 November* •

There's a wonderful bond between you and you-know-who today, bringing you closer together and adding depth to your relationship. A lot of what happens between you now will remain unspoken, which will add to the special atmosphere and convince you that you're on the same wavelength. If you meet someone new today, it will be almost impossible to get them out of your mind.

• *Tuesday 16 November* •

You're in the mood to get through a lot of work today, even if it's rather tedious or tricky. You're feeling efficient and practical, and just want to get on with the job in hand. There could be some good news about a forthcoming pay deal or bonus, even if it doesn't land in your lap immediately. You'll also forge a happy bond with a colleague or customer. A good day!

• *Wednesday 17 November* •

Someone is trying to do too much, so they're rushing around like a headless chicken and getting themselves into a right old state. Keep out of their way as much as possible; if you don't, you'll either get the sharp edge of their tongue or run the risk of being flattened as they stampede right over you. Take care if you catch their hectic mood, as it could make you rather accident-prone.

• Thursday 18 November •

Give your brain some exercise today, especially if you're analysing a situation or trying to understand a moral dilemma. You'll enjoy wrestling with big questions, and will have even more fun if you can discuss your conclusions with someone who shares your outlook on the world. There could also be an enjoyable contact with someone who lives a long way away.

• Friday 19 November •

You want to put your back into your work today, because it will give you a strong sense of satisfaction to know that you're doing everything to the best of your ability. Right now, you understand that you get what you give out, and that you can't expect to take with both hands if you aren't prepared to give in a similar fashion. And right now you want to give your all to the chores.

• Saturday 20 November •

Financial and emotional matters are fraught with difficulties today, caused partly by the tight-lipped attitude of a certain person and partly by your current tendency to feel hurt and ignored. It's a recipe for unhappiness unless you can distance yourself from the prevailing miserable mood and not let it ruin your day. Believe it or not, things aren't as bad as they seem.

• *Sunday 21 November* •

The astrological emphasis is firmly on relationships today, encouraging you to be receptive to the changes that are currently on the agenda and to approach them with generosity and resilience. Life should be easier during the next four weeks, because you will want to create harmonious atmospheres whenever possible and partners will respond accordingly.

• *Monday 22 November* •

Between now and mid-December you'll want to put a lot of effort into mundane chores and your general work. This will provide some welcome light relief if you're currently struggling over your relationship with you-know-who. If you're single and looking for a new mate, you could meet them through work or through a medical matter. Suddenly got the urge to visit the doctor?

• *Tuesday 23 November* •

Conversations go with a swing today, making it easy to put across your point of view. This is just what you need if you're having problems in making a certain so-and-so listen to a word you say without biting your head off. Set the tone by being friendly, positive and determined not to dredge up old history, and you'll encourage them to be equally chummy in return.

• *Wednesday 24 November* •

You're gripped by the sudden and urgent need to do your own thing and be seen as your own person today. You have no desire to fit in with other people, or to do things simply because they're expected of you. In fact, you're perfectly prepared to stick two fingers up to the world if necessary. This will certainly get your point across, but do you have to do something so drastic?

• *Thursday 25 November* •

You'll struggle if you're expected to concentrate on anything fiddly or complicated today because your mind simply won't be on the job. It's just one of those things, and unfortunately there won't be much you can do about it except to postpone anything really important until you're more in the mood to cope with it. Not possible? Then concentrate like mad and doublecheck everything you do.

• *Friday 26 November* •

Take note of the message of today's Full Moon because it's telling you to take a long, hard look at your life and cut out anything or anyone that no longer belongs in it. You've reached the end of the road as far as certain things are concerned and you're no longer prepared to pretend otherwise. It's a brave step that you're taking but right now you feel that you have no choice. So good luck, and keep looking towards a brighter future.

• *Saturday 27 November* •

Have you started your Christmas shopping yet or do you shudder to even think of it? Well, the shops are calling and you're starting to think about which presents you want to buy. Of course, you'll probably dream up a long present list of your own at the same time, but at least that means your loved ones will have some idea about what to buy you. So take a notebook with you!

• *Sunday 28 November* •

Keep your cool today or conversations will have a nasty habit of turning into ding-dong matches in which you're trying to score points off each other. You know that you have a very clever way with words, Gemini, but try to resist the temptation to descend into sarcasm or sour comments. You'll only have to apologize later on when you've calmed down.

• *Monday 29 November* •

Do you believe in the benefits of creative visualization? Let's hope so because it will work in some wonderful ways for you today. If you don't fancy that, then write down a list of everything you want to happen in your life and concentrate hard on turning them into reality. Some of your ideas may sound far-fetched to others but right now you're prepared to believe in them 100 per cent, and that's exactly what you should be doing.

• *Tuesday 30 November* •

Between now and 20 December you'll have to mind your Ps and Qs when talking to partners because there will be some glitches in your communications. For instance, you may misunderstand each other or you might not be able to make contact as often as you like. Be very careful not to imply things that you don't mean, or to give the wrong impression, because that will cause endless trouble.

DECEMBER AT A GLANCE

Love	♥ ♥ ♥ ♥ ♥
Money	£ $ £ $ £
Career	💻 💻 💻
Health	☼ ☼ ☼

• *Wednesday 1 December* •

Financial worries are never far away today, but try not to let them get out of control or you'll make yourself feel really fraught. If you're in a panic about how you're going to afford this very expensive month, you need to work out a strict budget. Above all, be realistic about what you can and can't do, and don't allow panic to lead you by the nose.

• *Thursday 2 December* •

This is a super day for doing something sociable, and if it's festive as well then so much the better. You'll enjoy mingling with friends, neighbours and partners, and may even get the chance to smooth over recent problems with a certain person. Right now you're making a big effort to get on well with everyone and it will be much appreciated.

• *Friday 3 December* •

You're normally pretty canny but today you're wearing a pair of rose-tinted spectacles that prevent you seeing what's really going on around you. There probably isn't much harm in this if your vision is only temporarily obscured but you could be heading for problems if you persist in taking a very idealistic view of a current situation. It's especially important that you're being realistic if someone's health is involved.

• *Saturday 4 December* •

You're full of empathy and compassion today, helping you to tune in to what's going on around you and to know instinctively if someone needs your support. You're also prepared to give someone a second chance or the opportunity to redeem themselves if they've recently let you down. At the moment you have no interest in holding grudges because you know you're bigger than that.

• *Sunday 5 December* •

Sparks will fly with a colleague if you're at work today, because there's a tremendous amount of nervous energy flowing between you. If your time is your own, you'll want to devote plenty of it to enjoyment and entertainment, preferably in the company of some of your favourite people. Can you find an excuse for throwing an impromptu party?

• *Monday 6 December* •

You're feeling practical and efficient today, particularly when it comes to keeping on top of the domestic chores and bills. It will give you pleasure to make sure that everything is ticking over nicely at home, and also to take any actions that might save you money. If you're doing some food shopping you'll be able to sniff out a bargain at fifty paces.

• *Tuesday 7 December* •

You're blessed with plenty of tact today, so put it to good use. There's little to fear if you're getting together with someone who isn't always the easiest company because you'll manage to charm them into being pleasant for a change. Just to add some sparkle to your day there could be an amusing flirtation with a certain person.

• *Wednesday 8 December* •

You're in the mood for a heart-to-heart with a certain someone today, and it will help to bring you closer together and increase your understanding of one another. This is also a golden opportunity to talk about any problems that have been rankling between you, and to get them out into the open so you can discuss them and then put them behind you.

• *Thursday 9 December* •

Beware of taking on too much because it will be an effort to get through it all. You might even have to give up the unequal struggle, which won't do much for your ego or your reputation. Be especially careful about this if you're at work, where a certain person may try to take advantage of what they see as your weakness or failure to deliver the goods.

• *Friday 10 December* •

If you were planning to get a lot done today you'd better lock yourself away from every other living soul. That's because it's a day when everyone you meet is immensely chatty, and you're also in a garrulous frame of mind. It's fine if you don't have anything else to do, but it will be frustrating if you're trying to get on with the chores and you keep being interrupted. Try to be considerate if someone else is up to their eyes in work and you're holding them up.

• *Saturday 11 December* •

It's another chatty day, and once again you'll enjoy a lovely long natter. However, try to bear in mind that you're in a very subjective mood at the moment so you're bound to see everything from your own standpoint. This will give you a very lop-sided view of the world, especially if you're thinking about some of your relationships.

• *Sunday 12 December* •

The coming fortnight is excellent for getting involved in any form of team work because you'll try hard to pull your weight without overshadowing anyone else. It's a very auspicious period for making an emotional commitment to someone or for doing your best to understand what makes a certain person tick.

• *Monday 13 December* •

The accent is firmly on partnerships at the moment and today you're able to get right down to the nuts and bolts of a particular relationship. You'll manage to cut through the distractions and expectations to discover what's really going on between the two of you, thereby offering you the chance to make positive changes and adjustments that will mean you get on better in 2005.

• *Tuesday 14 December* •

You're viewing the world from a wonderfully optimistic perspective today, which makes you feel good. However, it's important that you keep your feet on the ground and don't allow yourself to be carried away by wishful thinking or unrealistic expectations. These will lead you in the wrong direction and you'll be bitterly disappointed when reality intrudes on your lovely dreams.

• *Wednesday 15 December* •

You're in an expansive mood and are looking for activities that will complement your currently open-minded view of the world. Anything connected with travel or education is right up your street today, especially if you're planning for the future. The enticing prospect of arranging your next holiday may be too good to resist.

• *Thursday 16 December* •

During the next few weeks you'll be happiest when you're with people who make you feel loved and cherished. At times you'll bend over backwards to keep them sweet, and may even concede arguments and disputes for the sake of peace. Try not to make it peace at any price because that could mean setting up problems with partners who will then try to take advantage of your good nature. Co-operation is one thing, being a doormat is quite different.

• *Friday 17 December* •

Maybe it's the pre-Christmas tension but certain people will turn snappy in the blink of an eye today. This is especially likely if they've got a lot on their plate or they think they're very important, and you may have to treat them with kid gloves if you want to avoid getting sucked into a bad-tempered war of words. Some gentle humour may help to rescue the situation before it descends into acrimony.

• *Saturday 18 December* •

Grit your teeth because this will be a tricky day in which things don't go well. For a start, it seems that certain people are going out of their way to be difficult. Maybe an older relative is throwing their weight around and telling you what to do, making you long to tell them to take a running jump. The greater the gap between your ages or social status, the more irritated you'll be.

• *Sunday 19 December* •

Relationships are hard work this Sunday, thanks to certain people who are playing by their own rules and doing whatever they want, regardless of your feelings. You may also have to cope with a partner who needs more freedom than you're prepared to give them or who is finding other ways to wind you up. The more you react, the more you'll encourage them to be awkward.

• *Monday 20 December* •

As you've no doubt noticed, communications with partners haven't always been easy this December but they should start to straighten themselves out from today. As this is the season of goodwill to all men, you might want to smooth over any rough edges in your relationships by discussing what's gone wrong and working together to find sensible solutions.

• *Tuesday 21 December* •

Close relationships sometimes cause problems for you because the level of intimacy involved makes you feel uncomfortable. Yet this is precisely what you should concentrate on during the next four weeks, so do your best to let down your guard with partners and to reveal your true self, warts and all. Allow them to do the same in return.

• *Wednesday 22 December* •

If you're currently keeping something secret it will really start to prey on your mind today and you'll worry about blurting it out at the wrong moment. It's one of those days in which you're absent-minded and completely wrapped up in your own thoughts. As a result, it will be hard to concentrate on anything else and this won't go down well in certain quarters.

• *Thursday 23 December* •

You're in a very erratic mood today, making you feel restless, edgy and nervy. It may be almost impossible to settle to anything for long because you soon lose interest. If life becomes boring you'll want to liven it up in some way and it's highly likely that you'll choose the most disruptive and controversial option you can think of, even though you know this will cause trouble.

• *Friday 24 December* •

It's a busy day and you've got quite enough to do without having to cope with someone who is clamouring for your attention and likely to go into a huff if they don't get it. Is this person feeling neglected because you're busily occupied else-where, or are there other reasons for their demanding mood? Simply giving them a big hug could make all the difference to their behaviour.

• *Saturday 25 December* •

Happy Christmas! You're keen to make it a memorable day and you'll do your best to make it go with a swing. You're in a lively, excited mood and are really good company. You're also keen to ring the changes a bit and will want to bring some of your Christmas traditions up to date without spoiling things for everyone else. What do you have in mind?

• *Sunday 26 December* •

Today's Full Moon will affect your finances over the next two weeks, which isn't a very seasonal thought if you're already well aware that you've overspent this month. Be prepared to do some juggling or to seek expert advice if you're worried about how you're going to cope. It will also be a good opportunity to re-evaluate some of your values in life.

• *Monday 27 December* •

Let your imagination take you on a wonderful journey today, whether that means curling up with a good book, losing yourself in an adventure film or exercising your own creative talents. Don't discount any hunches or psychic flashes that come to you because they could be a lot more accurate than you imagine, particularly if they link you with people who live overseas.

• *Tuesday 28 December* •

You're in the perfect position to put your views across to partners today, because you're blessed with diplomacy and consideration for others. If you've been waiting for the right moment to tell a certain person how much they mean to you, speak up now while you're so silver-tongued and eloquent. You could also be on the receiving end of some delicious sweet nothings.

• *Wednesday 29 December* •

It's awfully easy to get distracted and confused because your mind is wandering about in all sorts of different directions. You're also in a highly impressionable state so will believe almost anything you're told now, whether it's true or a total flight of fancy. Be wary of muddling others by only telling them half the story or letting your imagination fill in any gaps.

• *Thursday 30 December* •

You shine in all social settings today and you'll quickly become the centre of attention. This will be highly gratifying, but even more so if you-know-who is plainly smitten by your many charms. If you're a solo Gemini you stand a good chance of meeting a new love now, so put on your best clothes and make a beeline for the nearest party or gathering. Good luck!

• *Friday 31 December* •

You'll need every ounce of patience today because even the best-laid plans could go up in smoke at a moment's notice. It seems that certain people are doing their best to throw spanners in the works, and the more annoyed you become the more they'll goad you still further. If there's dissent in the ranks about how to spend New Year's Eve, you may decide to go your own sweet way and prove that you're an individual in your own right. But try not to let any bad feelings mar the celebrations. Happy New Year!

YOUR GEMINI SUN SIGN

In this chapter I am going to tell you all about your Gemini Sun sign. But what is a Sun sign? It often gets called a star sign, but are they the same thing? Well, yes, although 'Sun sign' is a more accurate term. Your Sun sign is the sign that the Sun occupied when you were born. Every year, the Sun moves through the heavens and spends an average of 30 days in each of the twelve signs. When you were born, the Sun was moving through the sign of Gemini, so this is your Sun or star sign.

This chapter tells you everything you want to know about your Sun sign. To start off, I describe your general personality – what makes you tick. Then I talk about your attitude to relationships, the way you handle money, what your Sun sign says about your health and, finally, which careers are best for you. Put all that together and you will have a well-rounded picture of yourself.

 Character

Your quicksilver mind and high levels of nervous energy make you one of the liveliest members of the zodiac. You're unlikely to be one of those people who sit quietly in the corner, barely saying a word. If you are, you're probably taking note of what's going on in the interests of gossip, or so that you can re-member it all for your next novel. You belong to the element of Air, so you spend a lot of time in your head, thinking things through.

Your ruler, Mercury, is responsible for your mental agility and your seeming ability to be in several places at once. You certainly know what's going on around you! You're endlessly curious about life and really enjoy talking to people so you can discover what makes them tick. Mind you, you aren't always listening because you also enjoy chattering away, and you can be quite a gossip!

One of your greatest qualities is your versatility. You can turn your hand to almost anything. In fact, you're happiest when life offers you a lot of variety and you can quickly become fed up when things take on a rather monotonous flavour. You find it easy to fit into your surroundings and your bubbly personality helps you to get on well with others.

You thoroughly enjoy using your brain so you're probably a whizz at puzzles, crosswords and quizzes. You may even be so good at card games that lesser players refuse to play with you any more because they're so fed up with losing, especially if money is involved.

 **Relationships**

If you're a typical Gemini, you're very sociable and enjoy keeping in touch with your many friends. The arrival of the Internet has been heaven-sent for you because it means you can conduct a hectic correspondence with people all over the world without spending a fortune in the process. You like the idea of being able to contact so many people whenever it suits you.

It's often said that Geminis are fickle, and it's true that yours isn't a sign that's exactly renowned for its loyalty. Some Geminis enjoy playing the romantic field even after they've settled down with someone, but most prefer to indulge in some harmless flirting and to leave it at that.

When looking for a partner, it's vital that you choose someone who is a good match for you mentally. You'll soon get fed up with anyone who can't string two sentences together or whose eyes glaze over when you start discussing your favourite subjects. You're as appreciative of attractive people as anyone else, but very often it's brains rather than beauty that dictate your final choice of partner. If all you want is a pretty face, what's to stop you looking in the mirror?

Gemini is the sign of the Twins and many members of this sign go through life looking for their soulmate – that person who will make them feel complete. Their twin, in other words. What they don't realize is that this perfect person is inside them – it's another aspect of their own personality. Once you've discovered this for yourself, it will have a transformative effect on all your relationships because you won't be so dependent on other people any more.

Money

A Gemini and their money are soon parted. You can't resist the lure of shops, even if you're only going to buy the latest issue of a magazine. Money has a nasty habit of disappearing from your wallet at an alarming rate, simply because you're always buying things. And it soon adds up! You're the sort of person who will arrive at the airport armed with a book and a magazine to read on the flight, and who will then buy yourself a couple more books in the bookshop and several newspapers as well, just in case you get bored with your original choices.

The idea of keeping track of your money doesn't exactly make you want to rush off and scrutinize your bank statements right this minute. You usually prefer to take a more relaxed attitude, and often trust to luck that your bank and credit card companies have got their figures right. Even so, you may enjoy the idea of banking over the Internet, and could while away several happy hours setting up direct debits and other payments online.

Books, magazines and newspapers probably eat up quite a lot of your money. Gadgets and appliances may also make a big dent in your budget. You can't resist them! Computer notebooks, personal organizers, WAP phones and similar items could have been made for you. You also love computer programs that cater for your particular interests and you may be a big fan of computer games too. So many things to buy, so little time!

Health

The sign of Gemini rules the hands, arms and lungs, so it's important that you take extra care of these areas of your body. Most Geminis live on nervous energy and so the chances are that you need stimulants such as coffee, cigarettes and chocolate when your energy starts to flag. These will all help to keep you going during the day, especially if you don't think you've got time for a proper meal. Such a hectic lifestyle often means you have a wiry build and rarely have to worry about putting on weight.

Insomnia may be a problem for you, especially if you race through the day and don't have much time for yourself. The moment your head hits the pillow, your brain will start to process the day's events and you'll toss and turn half the night. Yet, strangely enough, you thrive on having a busy life. When things slow down and become predictable, you may start to feel lethargic and gloomy. You love it when you don't know what's going to happen next, even if you do complain about it at the time. Deep down, you adore feeling as though you've got your finger on the pulse and are at the centre of all the activity.

 **Career**

Any career that allows you to use your brain is a good choice! Your innate ability to communicate with others means you're a natural for a job in PR, market research, the media and retail. Sometimes you amaze yourself by the way you can talk off the top of your head about all sorts of things and manage to sound authoritative, even if you haven't got a clue what you're going on about! Whatever you do for a living, it's important that it allows you to express yourself in some way. And if your job doesn't give you that scope, you need to find it in other areas of your life, or you'll be a very frustrated Gemini indeed.

When you work with other people you can't help getting drawn into office politics. You love watching what's going on, deciding who fancies who and keeping track of the latest gossip-worthy developments. You may often be found hanging around the coffee machine, picking up a few titbits and filling everyone in on any details they might have missed. But you are also a very valuable member of the team because you're quick-witted, amusing and great company!

LOVE AND THE STARS

Have you ever noticed that you get on better with some signs than others? Perhaps all your friends belong to only a few signs or you've never hit it off with people who come from a particular sign. Or maybe you've recently met someone from a sign that you aren't familiar with at all, and you're wondering how your relationship will develop. Well, this chapter gives you a brief insight into your relationship with the other Sun signs. Check the combination under your own sign's heading first, then read about your relationship from the viewpoint of the other sign to find out what they think of you. It could be very revealing!

At the end of this chapter you'll find two compatibility charts that tell you, at a glance, how well you get on with the other signs as lovers and as friends. Look for the woman's Sun sign along the top of the chart and then find the man's sign down the side. The box where the two meet will show how well they get on together.

Even if your current relationship gets a low score from the charts, that doesn't mean it won't last. It simply indicates that you'll have to work harder at this relationship than at others.

♊ Gemini

Gemini and **Gemini** can be great fun or one big headache. You both crave variety and busy lives, but if you're both very sociable you may rarely see each other. Your sex life may also fizzle out over time.

Gemini and **Cancer** is tricky if you're lovers rather than friends. Although you'll adore your Cancerian's displays of affection at first, after a while they may seem rather clingy or will make you feel trapped.

Gemini and **Leo** have lots of fun together. You genuinely like and love one another, although you may secretly be amused sometimes by your Leo's regal behaviour and want to give them some gentle teasing.

Gemini and **Virgo** hit it off surprisingly well. There's so much for you to talk about and plenty of scope for having a good laugh. You're tremendous friends, whether your relationship is sexual or purely platonic.

Gemini and **Libra** is one of the most enjoyable combinations of all for you. You can encourage your easy-going Libran to be more assertive while they help you to relax, and also bring out the romance in your soul.

Gemini and **Scorpio** make uncomfortable bedfellows but good friends. You have very little in common sexually but are intrigued by each other's minds. You share an insatiable curiosity about human nature.

Gemini and **Sagittarius** have a really good time together. You especially enjoy learning new things from one another and never run out of things to talk about. Travel and books are just two of your many shared enthusiasms.

Gemini and **Capricorn** isn't very easy because you're so different. At first you're intrigued by your Capricorn's responsibility and common sense, but after a while they may seem a little staid or stuffy for you.

Gemini and **Aquarius** are fantastic friends. You're used to having the upper hand intellectually with people but here is someone who makes you think and encourages you to look at life in a new way.

Gemini and **Pisces** can be tricky because it's easy to hurt your Piscean's feelings without even realizing it. Neither of you is very keen on facing up to harsh reality, which causes problems if you both avoid dealing with the facts.

Gemini and **Aries** is tremendous fun and you'll spend a lot of time laughing. If even half the plans you make come to fruition, you'll have a fantastic time together with never a dull moment.

Gemini and **Taurus** can make you wonder what you're doing wrong. Your Taurean may seem bemused or even slightly alarmed by you, and positively threatened by your need for as much variety in your life as possible.

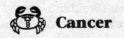 **Cancer**

Cancer and **Cancer** is wonderful because you're able to take refuge in each other. You'll lavish a lot of time and effort on your home. Problems will arise if one of you doesn't get on well with the other one's family or friends.

Cancer and **Leo** share a love of family life, and you may even agree to give it priority over everything else. You'll be very proud of your Leo's achievements but will fret if these take them away from home too often.

Cancer and **Virgo** have a lot to teach each other. You'll learn from your Virgo how to do things methodically and carefully, and you'll encourage them to be more demonstrative and loving. It should work well!

Cancer and **Libra** is great if you have shared goals. You both understand the importance of ambition and will readily support one another. You enjoy being with someone who isn't afraid to show their affection.

Cancer and **Scorpio** is a very emotional and satisfying pairing. You know you can reveal your true feelings to your Scorpio, and you'll encourage them to do the same with you. Sexually, you'll really be in your element.

Cancer and **Sagittarius** find it hard to appreciate each other. You may even feel as though you come from different planets because you operate on a very emotional level while your Sagittarian prefers to stick to the facts.

Cancer and **Capricorn** is a case of opposites attracting. You both need what the other one can offer, and you'll be especially pleased if your Capricorn's capacity for hard work will provide a roof over your head and a stable home.

Cancer and **Aquarius** can be quirky friends but you'll struggle to sustain an emotional relationship because you're chalk and cheese. Your need for love and reassurance may be very difficult for your Aquarian to deal with.

Cancer and **Pisces** are really happy together. It's great knowing that you're with someone who understands your deep emotional needs and your complicated personality. You'll also revel in taking care of your Piscean.

Cancer and **Aries** can work if you both make allowances for each other. You need to give your Aries a lot of freedom because they'll get very angry if they feel they're tied to your apron strings.

Cancer and **Taurus** is a marriage made in heaven. You both need a happy, comfortable home and you also share a love of food. Your relationship may be so self-sufficient that you barely need anyone else in your lives.

Cancer and **Gemini** is OK if you don't spend too much time together! You'll feel slightly threatened by your Gemini's need for an active and independent social life, and they'll resent being expected to spend so much time at home.

Leo

Leo and **Leo** is a very strong combination but there could be a few battles for power every now and then. After all, neither of you likes to relinquish the reins and hand over control to anyone else. Even so, you'll have a lot of fun.

Leo and **Virgo** is fine if you're prepared for some give and take but it won't be very easy if each of you stands your ground. You'll be pleased if your Virgo tries to help or advise you, but will be hurt if this turns to undue criticism.

Leo and **Libra** is a delicious pairing because it brings together the two signs of love. You'll adore being with someone who is so considerate, although their lack of decisiveness may sometimes make you grit your teeth with irritation.

Leo and **Scorpio** is wonderful until you have a row. At that point, you'll both refuse to budge an inch and admit that you might be in the wrong. You both set a lot of store by status symbols, which could work out expensive.

Leo and **Sagittarius** is great for keeping each other amused. You're both enthusiastic, intuitive and expansive, although you could sometimes be annoyed if your Sagittarian's social life prevents you seeing much of them.

Leo and **Capricorn** share a tremendous love of family and you'll enjoy creating a happy home together. Don't expect your Capricorn to be instinctively demonstrative: you may have to teach them to be more open.

Leo and **Aquarius** understand each other even if you don't always see eye to eye. Sometimes you can be left speechless by your plain-speaking Aquarian, and disappointed by their occasional reluctance to be cuddly.

Leo and **Pisces** bring out each other's creativity. This is a superb artistic partnership but may not be such good news if you're trying to maintain a sexual relationship because you have so little in common.

Leo and **Aries** have terrific fun together and will share many adventures. You'll enjoy making lots of plans, even if they don't always work out. You'll also spend plenty of money on lavishly entertaining your friends.

Leo and **Taurus** is the sort of relationship that makes you feel you know where you stand. You love knowing that your Taurean is steadfast and true, and that together you make a formidable team.

Leo and **Gemini** is a fun-filled combination that you really enjoy. You're stunned by your Gemini's endless inventiveness and their versatility, although you may secretly believe that they spread themselves too thin.

Leo and **Cancer** is great if you both need a comfortable and cosy home. But you may soon feel hemmed in if your Cancerian wants to restrict your social circle to nothing but family and close friends. You need more scope than that.

 Virgo

Virgo and **Virgo** can endure many storms together, even though it's tough going at times. Here is someone who completely understands your interesting mixture of quirky individualism and the need to conform.

Virgo and **Libra** get on well together up to a point but can then come unstuck. It annoys you when your Libran fails to stand up for themselves and you don't understand why they're so touchy when you point out their faults.

Virgo and **Scorpio** are both fascinated by the details of life and you'll spend many happy hours analysing people's characters. Try not to be too brusque when pointing out some of your Scorpio's stranger points; they won't like it!

Virgo and **Sagittarius** is a very sociable pairing and you'll enjoy being together. You'll also have some fascinating conversations in which you both learn a lot. Sexually, it will either be great or ghastly.

Virgo and **Capricorn** really understand each other. You appreciate your Capricorn's reliability but worry about their workaholic tendencies. You'll both benefit from being openly affectionate and loving with one another.

Virgo and **Aquarius** enjoy discussing just about everything under the sun. But you'll quickly get irritated by your Aquarian's idiosyncratic views and their insistence that they're always right. Surely if anyone's right, you are?

Virgo and **Pisces** is not the easiest combination you can choose. If your Piscean finds it hard to face up to reality, you won't be sympathetic because you simply can't understand such an ostrich-like attitude.

Virgo and **Aries** struggle to get on well as close partners. You simply don't understand each other. They make a mess and you like things to be tidy. They rush into things and you like to take your time. There is little common ground.

Virgo and **Taurus** love each other's company. You both like to keep your feet on the ground and you share a healthy respect for money. You also have a very raunchy time in the bedroom although you don't advertise that fact.

Virgo and **Gemini** is a super combination for friendship or business. You think along similar lines and both excel at being flexible. However, in a sexual relationship you may fail to appreciate each other's finer points.

Virgo and **Cancer** is a great team. You like to take care of worldly matters while your Cancerian creates a happy and cosy home. If they collect a lot of clutter you'll think of it as dust traps rather than delightful keepsakes.

Virgo and **Leo** find it hard to understand each other because you're so different. You may secretly find your Leo rather ostentatious and there could be rows about the amount of money they spend. Try to live and let live.

 Libra

Libra and **Libra** get on really well provided at least one of you is decisive and able to say what they think sometimes. You'll appreciate one another's consideration, sensitivity and intelligence. A great combination!

Libra and **Scorpio** are good friends but may not understand each other's sexual and emotional needs. You may feel uncomfortable with the brooding, intense moods of your Scorpio, wishing they took things less seriously.

Libra and **Sagittarius** have lots of fun together, especially when it comes to discussing ideas and taking off on jaunts. However, you could be rather nonplussed, and possibly even hurt, by your Sagittarian's blunt comments.

Libra and **Capricorn** get on famously if you share goals. You understand each other's need to work hard towards your ambitions. But you'll have to coax your Capricorn into being as demonstrative and loving as you'd like.

Libra and **Aquarius** appreciate one another's minds. You may be better friends than lovers, because you could be bemused and hurt if your Aquarian is unnerved by your need for romance and idealism.

Libra and **Pisces** share a need for peace and harmony. You'll adore being with someone who's so artistic and sensitive, but you both need to balance your romantic natures with hefty doses of reality every now and then.

Libra and **Aries** are a great example of how opposites can attract. You admire the way your brave Arien can be so outspoken, and they may even manage to teach you to stand up for yourself.

Libra and **Taurus** share a love of beauty and an appreciation of the finer things in life. At first you may think you've found your perfect partner, although you may get irritated if your Taurean is very placid.

Libra and **Gemini** get on well in every sort of relationship. You're amused by your Gemini's butterfly ability to flit from one topic to the next and will enjoy encouraging them to discover the romance that lurks inside them.

Libra and **Cancer** enjoy one another's company. You love the way your Cancerian so obviously cares about your welfare and happiness, and it does you good to be the one who's fussed over for a change.

Libra and **Leo** can be a very expensive combination! Neither of you is frightened to spend money and together you can have a field day. Emotionally, you revel in one another's company because you're both born romantics.

Libra and **Virgo** have to make a lot of effort to appreciate one another. You can understand the importance of attending to details but you may secretly think that your Virgo sometimes is too much of a nit-picker.

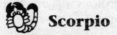 **Scorpio**

Scorpio and **Scorpio** feel safe with each other. You both know what you're capable of, good and bad. It's great to be with someone who matches you for intensity, but you might wind each other up and feed each other's neuroses.

Scorpio and **Sagittarius** can miss each other by miles. Even as friends, it's hard to understand one another. You like to zero in on the details while your Sagittarian prefers to take a broad view of the entire situation.

Scorpio and **Capricorn** bring out the best in one another, but it can take a little time. You enjoy the serious side to your Capricorn but you can also have some great laughs together. You also love knowing that they're so reliable.

Scorpio and **Aquarius** can have some terrific rows! You both have a tendency to be dogmatic and it's even worse when you get together. You can feel threatened if your Aquarian isn't as openly affectionate as you'd like.

Scorpio and **Pisces** share some powerful moments together. You love the complexity and sensitivity of your Piscean but will soon become suspicious if you think they're holding out on you or are playing games behind your back.

Scorpio and **Aries** is a tempestuous combination. Your temper builds up from a slow burn while your Arien will have a quick tantrum and then forget about it. Sexually, you'll have more than met your match.

Scorpio and **Taurus** complement each other in many ways. You're both loyal and loving, and you both need a secure home. However, problems will arise if one or both of you is possessive and jealous.

Scorpio and **Gemini** hit it off as friends but will struggle to stick together as lovers. You like to explore the nitty-gritty of situations while your Gemini apparently prefers to skim the surface. You may wonder if you can trust them.

Scorpio and **Cancer** can enjoy a highly emotional and satisfying relationship. You understand one another's needs and will take great delight in creating a stable and happy home life together.

Scorpio and **Leo** is tricky if you both want to rule the roost. Neither of you likes to relinquish control of situations, which can lead to some stormy battles for power. At times you may be jealous of your Leo's huge circle of friends.

Scorpio and **Virgo** have some wonderfully analytical conversations. You both enjoy digging below the surface to find out what's really going on. If it's a sexual relationship, its success will rest on what happens in the bedroom.

Scorpio and **Libra** appreciate one another but you may sometimes wish your Libran could be more forceful and dynamic. It will drive you mad when they sit on the fence or bend over backwards to please everyone.

🏹 Sagittarius

Sagittarius and **Sagittarius** will either have a whale of a time or never see each other. If you both have wide-ranging interests, it may be difficult to make enough time for one another and you may eventually drift apart.

Sagittarius and **Capricorn** think of each other as a creature from another planet. You like your Capricorn's common sense but will soon get fed up if they cling to tradition, are a workaholic or never want to take any risks.

Sagittarius and **Aquarius** have a fantastic time together. You share so many interests that there is always something to talk about, with some far-ranging discussions. But you may wish your Aquarian were less pedantic.

Sagittarius and **Pisces** enjoy being friends but it can be difficult to understand each other as lovers. You like your Piscean's sensitivity but wish they weren't quite so easily hurt when you make off-the-cuff comments.

Sagittarius and **Aries** is great fun. You'll have all sorts of adventures together, with exotic holidays a particular indulgence. You're both pretty outspoken and your no-holds-barred rows will raise the roof.

Sagittarius and **Taurus** struggle to hit it off. You're so different that it's hard to find much common ground. If your Taurean is possessive, you'll soon feel trapped and want to break free, or decide to do things behind their back.

Sagittarius and **Gemini** is a super combination. You have masses in common and are endlessly intrigued by one another.

However, you must be friends as well as lovers, otherwise you may soon get bored with each other.

Sagittarius and **Cancer** can't make each other out at all. You're mystified by your Cancerian's constant need for their home and family, and will be irritated if you think they're too parochial and unadventurous.

Sagittarius and **Leo** revel in each other's company, especially when it comes to having fun. This can be an expensive pairing because you both enjoy living it up whenever you get the chance. Shopping trips will also be costly.

Sagittarius and **Virgo** is OK up to a point. You enjoy each other's brains but you'll soon lose patience if your Virgo is very finicky and anxious. You like to let your hair down but they may always worry about the consequences.

Sagittarius and **Libra** like each other, whether as friends, family or lovers. You have enough similarities to find some common ground but enough differences to keep things interesting. It's an intriguing combination.

Sagittarius and **Scorpio** try and fail to understand each other. You like to take life as it comes and can't stand your Scorpio's tendency to plot things in advance. You'll hate it if they're suspicious or jealous of you.

Capricorn

Capricorn and **Capricorn** feel very safe together. At last you're with someone who understands you, and who's as reliable and responsible as you. However, this may mean that your work clashes with your relationship.

Capricorn and **Aquarius** is either a big hit or a big no-no. You both need to compromise and be willing to learn from each other for it to work. Your love of convention will be sorely challenged by your radical Aquarian.

Capricorn and **Pisces** can learn a lot from each other as friends. You'll learn to be more sensitive and open-minded. However, you'll soon be turned off if your Piscean is reluctant to face up to facts and be realistic.

Capricorn and **Aries** support each other in many ways. You're both ambitious and will respect one another's goals. You'll enjoy teaching your Arien to be more responsible, and they'll teach you how to play.

Capricorn and **Taurus** feel safe with one another. You both understand the importance of tradition and share the need to do things properly. You can get surprisingly earthy and intense in the bedroom.

Capricorn and **Gemini** don't really hit it off. You're amused by your Gemini but you may secretly think they're too flighty and superficial for you. It's difficult to find much common ground sexually or emotionally.

Capricorn and **Cancer** really enjoy each other's company. You both adore having someone to take care of, and if anyone can dissuade you from working round the clock it's a home-cooking, sensuous and affectionate Cancerian.

Capricorn and **Leo** both like the best in life but you won't be as willing to pay for it as your Leo. In fact, you may be seriously worried by their extravagance and also slightly wearied by their demanding social life.

Capricorn and **Virgo** go together like bread and butter. However, there may not be much jam if you're both careful with your money. If you share a home you'll want it to be traditional, with conventional family values.

Capricorn and **Libra** have a healthy respect for each other. You love your Libran's diplomacy and tact, because you know you can take them anywhere and they'll fit in. They'll also encourage you to open up emotionally.

Capricorn and **Scorpio** is a very businesslike pairing. You excel at making money together, no matter what your relationship. Sometimes you can be put off by the intense and complex passions of your Scorpio.

Capricorn and **Sagittarius** can be strange. You like each other for your curiosity value if not much else. Even so, your Sagittarian will teach you to be more broad-minded and relaxed, if you let them.

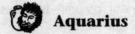 **Aquarius**

Aquarius and **Aquarius** is either wonderful or too much like hard work. One if not both of you must be willing to compromise sometimes, otherwise it will be continual stalemate. You'll have formidable battles of intellect.

Aquarius and **Pisces** is tricky. You don't understand each other, and the more unworldly and unrealistic your Piscean, the more dogmatic and precise you'll become in retaliation. You can easily hurt each other.

Aquarius and **Aries** are great sparring partners and you'll love every minute of it. Your Arien isn't afraid to stand up to you and to fight their corner. They'll also teach you a thing or two about sexual relationships.

Aquarius and **Taurus** is fine all the while you agree with each other. But, at the first hint of dissent, it will be war. Your need for emotional and intellectual freedom will clash with your Taurean's need for closeness.

Aquarius and **Gemini** are firm friends. You enjoy intense intellectual discussions and your Gemini will teach you to be more free-thinking and flexible. Try not to analyse your relationship out of existence.

Aquarius and **Cancer** can be an uneasy combination. You have little in common and don't understand each other. At first you'll enjoy being taken care of by your Cancerian but you may soon feel suffocated and trapped.

Aquarius and **Leo** enjoy each other's company. You love your Leo's exuberance and marvel at their social skills. You'll also be very impressed by their ability to organize you and make your life run so smoothly.

Aquarius and **Virgo** can seem like hard work. It's easier to be friends than lovers because you have such different views of the world. You enjoy pitting your wits against each other in wide-ranging discussions.

Aquarius and **Libra** is great fun and you love sharing ideas. If you get involved in an emotional relationship, your Libran will encourage you to be more demonstrative and less analytical about your feelings.

Aquarius and **Scorpio** is a very powerful combination because you're both so sure of yourselves. In the inevitable disputes, neither of you will want to back down. You may also be turned off by your Scorpio's complicated emotions.

Aquarius and **Sagittarius** enjoy each other's company. You also share a love of learning and both need as much intellectual freedom as you can get. This can be a very enduring relationship, whether it's platonic or passionate.

Aquarius and **Capricorn** will give you lots to think about because you'll be so busy trying to work out what makes each other tick. You may never arrive at an answer! You need to find some middle ground and to compromise.

 **Pisces**

Pisces and **Pisces** is wonderful if you're both prepared to face facts rather than pretend your relationship is something it's not. Your life is likely to be highly romantic and you'll love creating a sophisticated home together.

Pisces and **Aries** will be very trying at times. It may also be painful, since your Arien is unlikely to understand how easily you're hurt. Even so, they will encourage you to grow another layer of skin and to laugh at yourself.

Pisces and **Taurus** is a very sensual combination. You'll bring out the romantic in one another, but there will be times when you'll wish your Taurean were less matter-of-fact, practical and sensible.

Pisces and **Gemini** can have fun together but it's awfully easy for you to feel hurt by your Gemini's glib turns of phrase. You may be happier as friends than lovers because your emotional needs are so different.

Pisces and **Cancer** is super because you both express love in the same way. It's wonderful being with someone who takes such care of you, although your Cancerian may not understand your need to be left alone sometimes.

Pisces and **Leo** find it hard to understand each other. At times you may find your Leo rather grand. You share a pronounced artistic streak and you're both very affectionate, but is that enough to keep you together?

Pisces and **Virgo** can be difficult for you. Your Virgo may trample all over your feelings in their well-meaning efforts to point out your faults and help you to rise above them. It all sounds like a lot of unnecessary criticism to you.

Pisces and **Libra** can be incredibly romantic. You could easily have a heady affair straight out of a Hollywood weepie, but staying together is another matter. You may drift apart because you're reluctant to face up to problems.

Pisces and **Scorpio** is a highly emotional and complex pairing. You're both very deep and sensitive, and it may take a while before you begin to understand each other. Once that happens, you won't look back.

Pisces and **Sagittarius** is dicey because you won't know what to make of your forthright Sagittarian. Why are they so blunt? Can't they see that it upsets you? You may be better as friends who share lots of exploits.

Pisces and **Capricorn** is fine if your Capricorn is happy to show their feelings. But if they're buttoned up or repressed, you won't know how to get through to them. Even so, you'll love the way they provide for you.

Pisces and **Aquarius** may as well be talking different languages for all the sense you make to each other. They enjoy talking about ideas that leave you baffled but will struggle to express their emotions in the way you need.

 Aries

Aries and **Aries** is a very energetic combination, and you encourage each other in many different ways. Your relationship is competitive, sexy, exciting and sometimes pretty tempestuous!

Aries and **Taurus** can be difficult because you don't always understand each other. You love your Taurean's loyalty and affection but can feel frustrated if they're a great traditionalist or very stubborn.

Aries and **Gemini** get on like a house on fire and love hatching up new schemes together. But your differing sexual needs could cause problems, especially if your Gemini doesn't share your high sex drive.

Aries and **Cancer** is fine if your Cancerian will give you lots of personal freedom. However, they may be hurt if you aren't at home as much as they'd like, and they'll wonder what you're up to while you're away.

Aries and **Leo** really hit it off well and you'll have a lot of fun together. Sometimes you may wish your Leo would unbend a bit and be less dignified, but you adore the way they love and cherish you. It's great for your ego!

Aries and **Virgo** can be tricky because you have so little in common. You like to rush through life taking each day as it comes while they prefer to plan things in advance and then worry if they're doing the right thing. Irritating!

Aries and **Libra** have a lot to learn from each other. You enjoy the odd skirmish while your Libran prefers to keep the peace. Try to compromise over your differences rather than make them either/or situations.

Aries and **Scorpio** can be very dynamic and sexy together. Power is a huge aphrodisiac for you both so you're greatly attracted to each other. If you're a flirtatious Aries, your Scorpio will soon clip your wings.

Aries and **Sagittarius** are really excited by each other's company. You both adore challenges and will spur one another on to further feats and adventures. Your sex life is lively and interesting, and will keep you pretty busy.

Aries and **Capricorn** may not seem to have much in common on the surface. Yet you are both ambitious and will enjoy watching each other's progress. Sexually, things are surprisingly highly charged and naughty.

Aries and **Aquarius** have a lot of fun together but also share plenty of sparring matches. You get on better as friends than lovers because your Aquarian may not be nearly as interested in sex as you are.

Aries and **Pisces** is one of those tricky combinations that needs a lot of care if it's to succeed. It's horribly easy for you to upset your Piscean, often without realizing it, and you may get bored with having to reassure them so much.

🐂 **Taurus**

Taurus and **Taurus** is great because you're with someone who understands you inside out. Yet although this is comforting at first, it might start to become rather boring after a while, especially if you both like playing it safe.

Taurus and **Gemini** is good for keeping you on your toes, although you may find this tiring in the long term. They need a lot of change and variety, which can unsettle you and make you cling to stability and tradition.

Taurus and **Cancer** is lovely. You both appreciate the same sorts of things in life, such as good food, a loving partner and a cosy home. Once you get together you'll feel as though you've found your true soulmate.

Taurus and **Leo** share a love of luxury and the good things in life. You also know you can trust your Leo to be faithful and loyal, and in return you will shower them with plenty of admiration and moral support.

Taurus and **Virgo** is a very practical combination. Neither of you likes wasting time or money, although you may sometimes wish that your Virgo could be a little less austere and a bit more relaxed. But you still love them.

Taurus and **Libra** can have a very sensual and loving relationship. Neither of you likes conflict and you both need affectionate partners. But you may end up spending a lot of money together on all sorts of luxuries.

Taurus and **Scorpio** is a very powerful combination, especially in the bedroom. You both place a lot of importance on fidelity and loyalty, and you'll both believe that your relationship is the most important thing in your lives.

Taurus and **Sagittarius** don't really understand each other. You enjoy your home comforts and are generally content with life, while your Sagittarian always finds the grass is greener on the other side of the fence.

Taurus and **Capricorn** have a lot in common. You're both lusty, earthy and full of common sense. If you aren't careful, your relationship could get bogged down in practicalities, making you neglect the fun side of things.

Taurus and **Aquarius** struggle to appreciate each other. You enjoy sticking to the status quo whenever possible, while your Aquarian is always thinking of the future. You're both very stubborn, so rows can end in stalemate.

Taurus and **Pisces** is fine if your Piscean has their feet on the ground, because then you'll enjoy their sensitivity. But if they're very vague or other-worldly, you'll soon get annoyed and lose patience with them.

Taurus and **Aries** isn't the easiest combination for you. Although you enjoy your Arien's enthusiasm, it can wear a bit thin sometimes, especially when they're keen on something that you think is unrealistic or too costly.

Compatibility in Love and Sex at a glance

F M	♈	♉	♊	♋	♌	♍	♎	♏	♐	♑	♒	♓
♈	8	5	9	7	9	4	7	8	9	7	7	3
♉	6	8	4	10	7	8	8	7	3	8	2	8
♊	8	2	7	3	8	7	9	4	9	4	9	4
♋	5	10	4	8	6	5	6	8	2	9	2	8
♌	9	8	9	7	7	4	9	6	8	7	9	6
♍	4	8	6	4	4	7	6	7	7	9	4	4
♎	7	8	10	7	8	5	9	6	9	6	10	6
♏	7	9	4	7	6	6	7	10	5	6	5	7
♐	9	4	10	4	9	7	8	4	9	6	9	5
♑	7	8	4	9	8	6	8	4	4	8	4	5
♒	8	6	9	4	9	4	9	6	8	7	8	2
♓	7	6	7	9	6	7	6	9	7	5	4	9

1 = the pits
10 = the peaks

Key

♈ – Aries
♉ – Taurus
♊ – Gemini
♋ – Cancer
♌ – Leo
♍ – Virgo

♎ – Libra
♏ – Scorpio
♐ – Sagittarius
♑ – Capricorn
♒ – Aquarius
♓ – Pisces

Compatibility in Friendship at a glance

F M	♈	♉	♊	♋	♌	♍	♎	♏	♐	♑	♒	♓
♈	8	5	10	5	9	3	7	8	9	6	8	5
♉	6	9	6	10	7	8	7	6	4	9	3	9
♊	9	3	9	4	9	8	10	5	10	5	10	6
♋	6	9	4	9	5	4	6	9	4	10	3	9
♌	10	7	9	6	9	4	8	6	9	6	9	7
♍	5	9	8	4	4	8	5	8	8	10	5	6
♎	8	9	10	8	8	6	9	5	9	6	10	7
♏	7	8	5	8	7	7	6	9	4	5	6	8
♐	9	5	10	4	10	8	8	4	10	7	9	6
♑	6	9	5	10	6	9	5	5	4	9	5	6
♒	9	6	10	5	9	5	9	7	9	5	9	3
♓	6	7	6	10	6	8	7	9	8	6	4	10

1 = the pits
10 = the peaks

Key

♈ – Aries
♉ – Taurus
♊ – Gemini
♋ – Cancer
♌ – Leo
♍ – Virgo

♎ – Libra
♏ – Scorpio
♐ – Sagittarius
♑ – Capricorn
♒ – Aquarius
♓ – Pisces

YOUR ASTROLOGICAL HOLIDAY GUIDE

Have you ever wondered which holiday destination is right for your Sun sign, and what sort of activities you'll most enjoy when you get there? Well, your questions have been answered because this guide will give you some great ideas about how to have the holiday of a lifetime.

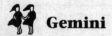 **Gemini**

Variety is the spice of life for you, so you won't want to visit the same destination year after year. Instead, you like the thought of trying somewhere completely different each time, because half the fun is reading about it before you go and then trying to cram a selection of indispensable travel guides and phrase books into your already bulging suitcase. You need to keep on the move, too, so are happiest if the local transport is excellent or you can hire a car to get around. You're thrilled by bustling cities, especially if you can sit in a café and watch the world go by, then shop to your heart's content. Destinations that are steeped in history or culture also appeal to you. Another option is to take an activity holiday in which you'll learn something new; it could be anything from watercolour painting to belly-dancing.

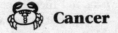

Cancer

Familiarity breeds content for you, so you can feel uneasy when visiting somewhere for the first time. What if you don't like it? You're the sort of person who is welcomed with open arms by hoteliers because if you like the place you'll return year after year, and you'll take your nearest and dearest with you. It's a rare Cancerian who doesn't enjoy eating, so you'll want to choose a destination in which the food is to your liking, and you'll hope that there's lots of it. You can't cope with anything too exotic or strange, and you need to take care of your sensitive tummy, which rules out some of the more far-flung corners of the world. You also can't tolerate extreme heat or humidity. You love being near water and would enjoy a relaxing beach holiday or staying at a hotel on a large lake. Another option is a self-catering holiday in which you can create a home from home.

Leo

The one thing you crave above all else is sunshine, so it's very high up on your list of holiday priorities. You really come into your own when you're in a hot climate, although even you will wilt if the temperature rises too high. If you could have your heart's desire, you'd stay in a luxurious and exclusive resort on a tropical island, where you could do lots of celebrity-spotting while sipping cocktails on a palm-fringed beach. Too expensive? Then you would love going on safari and seeing your namesake lions prowling around, provided you didn't have to hammer in your own tent pegs every night. You do have your standards! Something else that would appeal is driving through a warm and friendly country in a chic or classic car, staying at delightful hotels along the way and buying lots of lovely clothes to wear when you get home.

 Virgo

Although you may sound enthusiastic when your friends tell you about their trips to exotic locations, or describe meals containing the sort of wriggly items that you would squash to death if you found them in your garden, in reality you avoid them like the plague. Actually, you would probably rather have the plague than visit anywhere with dodgy hygiene, unsafe drinking water, poisonous creepy-crawlies, stomach-churning food or primitive plumbing. You're not the most adventurous traveller in the world and you don't care! Ideal holiday destinations for you include ski resorts where you can get exercise, hot chocolate and fresh air, or luxurious health farms that serve more than just a single lettuce leaf once a day. You would also adore a specialist holiday which caters for one of your interests and keeps your very clever brain fully occupied.

Libra

You can take any amount of luxury, relaxation and lotus-eating, especially when you're on holiday. You're too intelligent to be content spending a fortnight lying on a beach, but you might fancy visiting somewhere that offers the twin attractions of sparkling blue seas and plenty of culture. Decent food will also be high on your list of holiday essentials, because there's nothing you like better than working your way through a menu full of delicious temptations. You may even choose your destination or hotel purely on the strength of its cuisine or wine, and you'll do your best to sample as much of it as possible. If you're a typical Libran you have very sophisticated tastes and would enjoy visiting one of the great cities of the world, especially if you can combine sightseeing with an enjoyable tour of the best shops you can find.

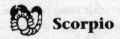 Scorpio

You take such an intense approach to life that regular breaks are essential for you, because they help you to get things back in perspective. What's more, you're prepared to spend quite a lot of money on a holiday if necessary. If you can only take a short break, you adore the thought of staying in a fabulous country hotel, complete with spa, swimming pool, gardens and Michelin-starred dining room. So what if the bill makes your eyes water? You'll have had more than your money's worth in terms of enjoyment. You soon get bored if nothing is going on, so an activity holiday is perfect for you, especially if it offers plenty of excitement. You could learn to scuba-dive, brush up your skiing, go potholing or practise body-surfing. If you fancy something less daredevil, you might consider a wine-tasting holiday, a murder-mystery weekend or an Antarctic cruise.

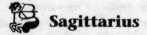 **Sagittarius**

If you're a dyed-in-the-wool Sagittarian, you've probably already chosen the destinations of your next ten holidays. Travel is in your blood and you love exploring the world. You're unlikely to want to revisit the same place twice, although you might develop an abiding passion for a particular country and enjoy visiting different parts of it over the years. In the end, you'll be quite an expert on the subject. Your ideal holiday offers a combination of delicious food and drink, breathtaking scenery, comfortable sleeping arrangements, plenty of history, loads of culture and lots to look at. Grilling on a beach for two weeks, looking only at the sand, is your idea of hell. You'd much rather jump on a local bus and see where it takes you, laze the afternoon away in a restaurant or put your guidebook through its paces. You enjoy both heat and cold, which means you can be happy almost anywhere in the world.

 **Capricorn**

You aren't entirely convinced by the need for holidays because they can seem like such an extravagance to you. Deep down, you'd probably rather stay at home and feel good about the money you've saved. If you are persuaded to go away, you

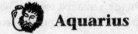

won't want to throw your cash around willy-nilly and will choose somewhere that doesn't cost the earth. Nevertheless, you aren't keen on places that are too cheap and cheerful, and you're quite choosy about the company you keep. You might enjoy a skiing holiday, rock climbing or simply relaxing high in the mountains somewhere. You're very practical, so would also appreciate a holiday in which you learn a new skill or craft. You have a strong conservative streak, so will avoid anywhere that's too exotic, strange or dangerous. Instead, you'll choose places that feel familiar, and preferably where there's no language barrier.

Aquarius

The last thing you want to do on holiday is be surrounded by crowds and feel that you're part of a gigantic marketing machine. Instead, you're drawn to places that are off the beaten track, unfashionable (so you don't have to rub shoulders with every Tom, Dick and Harry) or are yet to be discovered by most people. You have no interest in simple beach holidays, unless you can alternate sunbathing with plenty of sightseeing. Destinations steeped in history and culture are ideal for you, because you love tuning in to the atmosphere and learning more about the country you're visiting. It's also essential that the place offers peace and quiet, so you can read all those books you've brought with you. For you, part of the pleasure of going on holiday is meeting the locals, so it's important that you visit somewhere friendly and welcoming.

🦀 Pisces

You're so sensitive to atmospheres that you need to choose your holiday destination very carefully. Try to avoid political trouble spots or places that are heaving with fellow holiday-makers because your delicate nerves will soon become jangled and you'll start longing to go home again. You adore being near water, whether it's a lake or an ocean, and find it very relaxing just to listen to the sound of the waves while gazing into space. The clear blue waters of a tropical island would be paradise for you, because you love swimming. You aren't comfortable if you have to rough it, so are happiest staying somewhere that offers plenty of luxury. However, you'll be very disturbed if there's a marked contrast between your level of comfort and that of the local people. Your ideal holiday includes plenty of sightseeing, because you love soaking up the atmosphere and getting a strong sense of the spirit of the place.

🐏 Aries

In an ideal world, you would never visit the same holiday destination twice because you hate that sense of 'been there, done that'. Besides, there's a whole world out there waiting to be explored, so why waste your valuable holiday time going back to the same old resort year after year? If you're a typical Arien, excitement, heat and plenty of action are the ingredients for a perfect holiday. If a little courage is required, then so much the better. You'll enjoy regaling your friends and family with eye-popping tales of your bravery as you mastered white-water rafting, braved huge rollers on your surfboard, went on safari, trekked through a jungle or endured the baking heat of a desert. If you have to choose something that you consider to be more tame, you'll enjoy a fly-drive or activity holiday. At a pinch, you might be persuaded to lie on a beach but you won't want to do it for long because you'll soon get bored.

 **Taurus**

As the great hedonist of the zodiac, your idea of a blissful holiday is one in which you do as little as possible while other people attend to your every whim. If money is no object you'll be in seventh heaven staying in a luxury hotel that serves delectable drinks, sumptuous food and has the finest cotton sheets. Some signs are completely incapable of sitting around doing nothing but you could turn it into an art form, given half a chance. If you have to lower your holiday sights through a lack of cash, you'd enjoy staying in a self-catering cottage in beautiful surroundings. The cottage must have all mod cons, of course, because the charm of pumping your own water from a tumbledown well would pall after the first ten minutes. You feel revived and rejuvenated when you're surrounded by nature and beauty, so you might enjoy a holiday tour of famous gardens, a visit to a country renowned for its autumn colours or a trip to an unspoilt island paradise.

BORN ON THE CUSP?

Were you born on the cusp of Gemini – at the beginning or end of the sign? If so, you may have spent years wondering which sign you belong to. Are you a Gemini, a Taurean or a Cancerian? Different horoscope books and columns can give different dates for when the Sun moves into each sign, leaving you utterly confused. Yet none of these dates is wrong, as you'll discover in a minute. Checking your birth date, and time if you know it, in the list given in this chapter will allow you to solve the mystery at long last!

Many people believe that the Sun moves like clockwork from one sign to another on a specific day each year. But this isn't always true. For instance, let's look at the dates for the sign of Gemini. On the cover of this book I give them as 22 May to 21 June. Very often, the Sun will obediently change signs on these days but sometimes it won't. It can move from Taurus into Gemini on 20, 21 or 22 May and it can move into Cancer on 20, 21 or 22 June.

So how can you find out which sign you belong to if you were born on the cusp of Gemini? The only information you need is the place, year, day and the time of your birth if you know it. It helps to have the time of birth because if the Sun did move signs on your birthday, you can see whether it moved before or after you were born. If you don't have an exact time, even knowing whether it was morning or afternoon can be a help. For instance, if you were born in the morning and the Sun didn't move signs on your birthday until the afternoon, that will be enough information to tell you which sign is yours.

You need to know the place in case you were born outside the United Kingdom and have to convert its local time zone to British time. This information is easily available in many diaries and reference books.

Four Simple Steps to Find your Sun Sign

1 Write down the year, day, time and place of your birth, in that order.
2 If you were born outside the United Kingdom, you must convert your birth date and time to British time by adding or subtracting the relevant number of hours from your birth time to convert it to British time. This may take your birthday into the following day or back to the previous day. If so, write down this new date and time because that will be the one you use in the following calculations. If summer time was operating you must deduct the relevant number of hours to convert your birth time to Greenwich Mean Time (GMT).
3 If you were born in Britain, look up your year of birth in the list of British Summer Time (BST) changes to see if BST was operating when you were born. If it was, subtract the appropriate number of hours from your birth time to convert it to GMT. This may give you a different time and/or date of birth.
4 Look up your year of birth in the Annual Sun Sign Changes list. If you were born within these dates and times, you are a Gemini. If you were born outside them, you are either a Taurean if you were born in May, or a Cancerian if you were born in June.

Two Examples

Here are a couple of examples so you can see how the process works. Let's say we're looking for the Sun sign of Margaret, who was born in the UK on 22 May 1947 at 00:55. Start by checking the list of British Summer Time (BST) dates to see if BST was operating at the time of her birth. It was, but you will see that she was born during a phase when two hours had been added, so you have to subtract two hours from her birth time to convert it to GMT. This gives her a birth time of 22:55 on the previous day – therefore, her GMT birthday is 21 May and her GMT birth time is 22:55. Write this down, so you don't forget it. Now turn to the Annual Sun Sign Changes list and look up 1947, her year of birth. In that year, the Sun moved into Gemini on 21 May at 22:10, and Margaret was born at 22:55 GMT on that day, so she is definitely a Gemini. However, if she had been born on 21 May 1947 at 22:09 GMT, the Sun would still have been in Taurus (it didn't move into Gemini until 22:10) so she would be a Taurean.

But what would her sign be if she were born on 21 June 1957 at 18:55? First, check the dates in the BST list (note the year change from the above example). You will see she was born during a period when one hour had been added for BST, so you must subtract one hour to convert her birth time to GMT. This changes it to 17:55 on 21 June. Write this down. Now look up the Sun sign dates for 1957. This time, look at the June date. The Sun was in Gemini until 21 June at 16:20. So Margaret's GMT birth time was after the Sun had entered Cancer, making her a Cancerian.

Dates for British Summer Time

If your birthday falls within these dates and times, you were born during BST and will have to convert your birth time back to GMT. To do this, subtract one hour from your birth time. If you were born during a period that is marked *, you must subtract two hours from your birth time to convert it to GMT. All times are given in BST, using the 24-hour clock.

1920 28 Mar, 02:00–25 Oct, 01:59 inc
1921 3 Apr, 02:00–3 Oct, 01:59 inc
1922 26 Mar, 02:00–8 Oct, 01:59 inc
1923 22 Apr, 02:00–16 Sep, 01:59 inc
1924 13 Apr, 02:00–21 Sep, 01:59 inc
1925 19 Apr, 02:00–4 Oct, 01:59 inc
1926 18 Apr, 02:00–3 Oct, 01:59 inc
1927 10 Apr, 02:00–2 Oct, 01:59 inc
1928 22 Apr, 02:00–7 Oct, 01:59 inc
1929 21 Apr, 02:00–6 Oct, 01:59 inc
1930 13 Apr, 02:00–5 Oct, 01:59 inc
1931 19 Apr, 02:00–4 Oct, 01:59 inc
1932 17 Apr, 02:00–2 Oct, 01:59 inc
1933 9 Apr, 02:00–8 Oct, 01:59 inc
1934 22 Apr, 02:00–7 Oct, 01:59 inc
1935 14 Apr, 02:00–6 Oct, 01:59 inc
1936 19 Apr, 02:00–4 Oct, 01:59 inc
1937 18 Apr, 02:00–3 Oct, 01:59 inc
1938 10 Apr, 02:00–2 Oct, 01:59 inc
1939 16 Apr, 02:00–19 Nov, 01:59 inc
1940 25 Feb, 02:00–31 Dec, 23:59 inc
1941 1 Jan, 00:00–4 May, 01:59 inc
1941 4 May, 02:00–10 Aug, 01:59 inc*
1941 10 Aug, 02:00–31 Dec, 23:59 inc
1942 1 Jan, 00:00–5 Apr, 01:59 inc
1942 5 Apr, 02:00–9 Aug, 01:59 inc*
1942 9 Aug, 02:00–31 Dec, 23:59 inc
1943 1 Jan, 00:00–4 Apr, 01:59 inc
1943 4 Apr, 02:00–15 Aug, 01:59 inc*
1943 15 Aug, 02:00–31 Dec, 23:59 inc
1944 1 Jan, 00:00–2 Apr, 01:59 inc
1944 2 Apr, 02:00–17 Sep, 01:59 inc*
1944 17 Sep, 02:00–31 Dec, 23:59 inc
1945 1 Jan, 00:00–2 Apr, 01:59 inc
1945 2 Apr, 02:00–15 Jul, 01:59 inc*
1945 15 Jul, 02:00–7 Oct, 01:59 inc
1946 14 Apr, 02:00–6 Oct, 01:59 inc
1947 16 Mar, 02:00–13 Apr, 01:59 inc
1947 13 Apr, 02:00–10 Aug, 01:59 inc*
1947 10 Aug, 02:00–2 Nov, 01:59 inc
1948 14 Mar, 02:00–31 Oct, 01:59 inc

1949 3 Apr, 02:00–30 Oct, 01:59 inc
1950 16 Apr, 02:00–22 Oct, 01:59 inc
1951 15 Apr, 02:00–21 Oct, 01:59 inc
1952 20 Apr, 02:00–26 Oct, 01:59 inc
1953 19 Apr, 02:00–4 Oct, 01:59 inc
1954 11 Apr, 02:00–3 Oct, 01:59 inc
1955 17 Apr, 02:00–2 Oct, 01:59 inc
1956 22 Apr, 02:00–7 Oct, 01:59 inc
1957 14 Apr, 02:00–6 Oct, 01:59 inc
1958 20 Apr, 02:00–5 Oct, 01:59 inc
1959 19 Apr, 02:00–4 Oct, 01:59 inc
1960 10 Apr, 02:00–2 Oct, 01:59 inc
1961 26 Mar, 02:00–29 Oct, 01:59 inc
1962 25 Mar, 02:00–28 Oct, 01:59 inc
1963 31 Mar, 02:00–27 Oct, 01:59 inc
1964 22 Mar, 02:00–25 Oct, 01:59 inc
1965 21 Mar, 02:00–24 Oct, 01:59 inc
1966 20 Mar, 02:00–23 Oct, 01:59 inc
1967 19 Mar, 02:00–29 Oct, 01:59 inc
1968 18 Feb, 02:00–31 Dec, 23:59 inc
1969 1 Jan, 00:00–31 Dec, 23:59 inc
1970 1 Jan, 00:00–31 Dec, 23:59 inc
1971 1 Jan, 00:00–31 Oct, 01:59 inc
1972 19 Mar, 02:00–29 Oct, 01:59 inc
1973 18 Mar, 02:00–28 Oct, 01:59 inc
1974 17 Mar, 02:00–27 Oct, 01:59 inc
1975 16 Mar, 02:00–26 Oct, 01:59 inc
1976 21 Mar, 02:00–24 Oct, 01:59 inc
1977 20 Mar, 02:00–23 Oct, 01:59 inc
1978 19 Mar, 02:00–29 Oct, 01:59 inc
1979 18 Mar, 02:00–28 Oct, 01:59 inc
1980 16 Mar, 02:00–26 Oct, 01:59 inc
1981 29 Mar, 01:00–25 Oct, 00:59 inc
1982 28 Mar, 01:00–24 Oct, 00:59 inc
1983 27 Mar, 01:00–23 Oct, 00:59 inc
1984 25 Mar, 01:00–28 Oct, 00:59 inc
1985 31 Mar, 01:00–27 Oct, 00:59 inc
1986 30 Mar, 01:00–26 Oct, 00:59 inc
1987 29 Mar, 01:00–25 Oct, 00:59 inc
1988 27 Mar, 01:00–23 Oct, 00:59 inc
1989 26 Mar, 01:00–29 Oct, 00:59 inc

1990 25 Mar, 01:00–28 Oct, 00:59 inc
1991 31 Mar, 01:00–27 Oct, 00:59 inc
1992 29 Mar, 01:00–25 Oct, 00:59 inc
1993 28 Mar, 01:00–24 Oct, 00:59 inc
1994 27 Mar, 01:00–23 Oct, 00:59 inc
1995 26 Mar, 01:00–22 Oct, 00:59 inc
1996 31 Mar, 01:00–27 Oct, 00:59 inc
1997 30 Mar, 01:00–26 Oct, 00:59 inc

1998 29 Mar, 01:00–25 Oct, 00:59 inc
1999 28 Mar, 01:00–31 Oct, 00:59 inc
2000 26 Mar, 01:00–29 Oct, 00:59 inc
2001 25 Mar, 01:00–28 Oct, 00:59 inc
2002 31 Mar, 01:00–27 Oct, 00:59 inc
2003 30 Mar, 01:00–26 Oct, 00:59 inc
2004 28 Mar, 01:00–31 Oct, 00:59 inc

* Subtract two hours from the birth time to convert it to GMT.

Annual Sun Sign Changes

If your birthday falls within these dates and times, you are a Gemini. If you were born in May before the first date and time, you are a Taurean. If you were born in June after the second date and time, you are a Cancerian. All times are given in GMT, using the 24-hour clock.

1920 21 May, 09:22–21 Jun, 17:39 inc
1921 21 May, 15:17–21 Jun, 23:35 inc
1922 21 May, 21:11–22 Jun, 05:26 inc
1923 22 May, 02:46–22 Jun, 11:02 inc
1924 21 May, 08:41–21 Jun, 16:59 inc
1925 21 May, 14:33–21 Jun, 22:49 inc
1926 21 May, 20:15–22 Jun, 04:29 inc
1927 22 May, 02:08–21 Jun, 10:22 inc
1928 21 May, 07:53–21 Jun, 16:06 inc
1929 21 May, 13:48–21 Jun, 22:00 inc
1930 21 May, 19:42–22 Jun, 03:52 inc
1931 22 May, 01:16–22 Jun, 09:27 inc
1932 21 May, 07:07–21 Jun, 15:22 inc
1933 21 May, 12:57–21 Jun, 21:11 inc
1934 21 May, 18:35–22 Jun, 02:47 inc
1935 22 May, 00:25–22 Jun, 08:37 inc
1936 21 May, 06:08–21 Jun, 14:22 inc
1937 21 May, 11:58–21 Jun, 20:11 inc
1938 21 May, 17:51–22 Jun, 02:03 inc
1939 21 May, 23:27–22 Jun, 07:39 inc
1940 21 May, 05:23–21 Jun, 13:36 inc
1941 21 May, 11:23–21 Jun, 19:33 inc
1942 21 May, 17:09–22 Jun, 01:16 inc
1943 21 May, 23:03–22 Jun, 07:12 inc
1944 21 May, 04:51–21 Jun, 13:02 inc

1945 21 May, 10:41–21 Jun, 18:52 inc
1946 21 May, 16:34–22 Jun, 00:44 inc
1947 21 May, 22:10–22 Jun, 06:18 inc
1948 21 May, 03:58–21 Jun, 12:10 inc
1949 21 May, 09:51–21 Jun, 18:02 inc
1950 21 May, 15:28–21 Jun, 23:36 inc
1951 21 May, 21:16–22 Jun, 05:24 inc
1952 21 May, 03:04–21 Jun, 11:12 inc
1953 21 May, 08:53–21 Jun, 16:59 inc
1954 21 May, 14:48–21 Jun, 22:54 inc
1955 21 May, 20:25–22 Jun, 04:31 inc
1956 21 May, 02:13–21 Jun, 10:23 inc
1957 21 May, 08:11–21 Jun, 16:20 inc
1958 21 May, 13:52–21 Jun, 21:56 inc
1959 21 May, 19:43–22 Jun, 03:49 inc
1960 21 May, 01:34–21 Jun, 09:42 inc
1961 21 May, 07:23–21 Jun, 15:30 inc
1962 21 May, 13:17–21 Jun, 21:24 inc
1963 21 May, 18:59–22 Jun, 03:04 inc
1964 21 May, 00:50–21 Jun, 08:56 inc
1965 21 May, 06:51–21 Jun, 14:55 inc
1966 21 May, 12:33–21 Jun, 20:33 inc
1967 21 May, 18:19–22 Jun, 02:22 inc
1968 21 May, 00:07–21 Jun, 08:13 inc
1969 21 May, 05:50–21 Jun, 13:55 inc

1970 21 May, 11:38–21 Jun, 19:42 inc
1971 21 May, 17:16–22 Jun, 01:19 inc
1972 20 May, 23:00–21 Jun, 07:07 inc
1973 21 May, 04:55–21 Jun, 13:00 inc
1974 21 May, 10:37–21 Jun, 18:37 inc
1975 21 May, 16:24–22 Jun, 00:26 inc
1976 20 May, 22:22–21 Jun, 06:24 inc
1977 21 May, 04:15–21 Jun, 12:14 inc
1978 21 May, 10:09–21 Jun, 18:09 inc
1979 21 May, 15:55–21 Jun, 23:56 inc
1980 20 May, 21:43–21 Jun, 05:48 inc
1981 21 May, 03:40–21 Jun, 11:45 inc
1982 21 May, 09:24–21 Jun, 17:23 inc
1983 21 May, 15:07–21 Jun, 23:09 inc
1984 20 May, 20:59–21 Jun, 05:02 inc
1985 21 May, 02:44–21 Jun, 10:44 inc
1986 21 May, 08:29–21 Jun, 16:30 inc
1987 21 May, 14:11–21 Jun, 22:11 inc

1988 20 May, 19:58–21 Jun, 03:56 inc
1989 20 May, 15:29–20 Jun, 02:39 inc
1990 21 May, 07:38–21 Jun, 15:33 inc
1991 21 May, 13:21–21 Jun, 21:19 inc
1992 20 May, 19:13–21 Jun, 03:14 inc
1993 21 May, 01:03–21 Jun, 09:00 inc
1994 21 May, 06:49–21 Jun, 14:48 inc
1995 21 May, 12:35–21 Jun, 20:34 inc
1996 20 May, 18:24–21 Jun, 02:24 inc
1997 21 May, 00:19–21 Jun, 08:20 inc
1998 21 May, 06:06–21 Jun, 14:03 inc
1999 21 May, 11:53–21 Jun, 19:49 inc
2000 20 May, 17:50–21 Jun, 01:48 inc
2001 20 May, 23:45–21 Jun, 07:38 inc
2002 21 May, 05:30–21 Jun, 13:24 inc
2003 21 May, 11:13–21 Jun, 19:11 inc
2004 20 May, 17:00–21 Jun, 00:57 inc